THE DOGMATIC
Imagination

To Ramona
& Colin.

In memory
of your visit.

April 10/09

Jim R.

THE DOGMATIC
Imagination

The
Dynamics
of Christian
Belief

A. JAMES REIMER

Foreword by Raylene Hinz-Penner

Herald
Press

Waterloo, Ontario
Scottdale, Pennsylvania

National Library of Canada Cataloging-in-Publication Data
Reimer, A. James
    The dogmatic imagination : the dynamics of Christian belief /
A. James Reimer.
ISBN 0-8361-9246-X
    1. Theology, Doctrinal. I. Title.
BT21.3.R43 2003   230   C2003-901543-2

THE DOGMATIC IMAGINATION
Copyright © 2003 by Herald Press, Scottdale, Pa. 15683
    Published simultaneously in Canada by Herald Press,
    Waterloo, Ont. N2L 6H7. All rights reserved
Library of Congress Control Number: 2003103368
Canadiana Entry Number: C2003-901543-2
International Standard Book Number: 0-8361-9246-X

Printed in the United States of America
Book cover and design by Beth Oberholtzer
Front cover etching: The Ancient of Days by William Blake
(1757–1827). Whitworth Art Gallery, The University of Manchester,
UK/Bridgeman Art Library.

10 09 08 07 06 05 04 03 10 9 8 7 6 5 4 3 2 1

To order or request information, please call
1-800-759-4447 (individuals); 1-800-245-7894 (trade).
Website: www.heraldpress.com

To my children,
and children's children.

CONTENTS

FOREWORD

How does the movie line go? "You had me at 'hello'"?

Reimer had me at the first essay: faith is like Scrabble. He had me with his defense of catechism, that little book of 200 questions on big, big subjects for sixteen-year-olds: Mennonite beliefs about God, creation, sin and the Fall, heaven, hell. . . .

Reimer is right: we are wrong to believe that young people don't care about these issues. In my own case, the "unpardonable sin" was my catechism torture. I was sure that I had committed it and agonized until I went, in total dejection, to visit my minister, confess, and find out if hell was, indeed, my definite destination. That encounter was the most wonderful faith experience of my early years, one I have wrestled into poetry several times over the years. It was a faith adventure, demanding my youthful mind to stay with the preacher, especially as he tried to teach me irony, "Don't you understand that if you had committed the unpardonable sin, the hardening of the heart toward God's call, you wouldn't be in this office today?" Powerful, teachable faith moments rise up out of offering up big questions to youthful imagination, youthful passions, a keen desire to know.

Reimer's little essays are engaging in a kind of Kathleen Norris literary way; they trust the imagination to preserve faith. Our failure to entertain and engage faith issues is a failure of the imagination. And, because language is the product of imagination, our failure to engage faith is a failure of imagination and language. Faith is a Scrabble game, Reimer offers, not a puzzle. There is a fixed game board with an unalterable alphabet. There are rules. There is the luck of the draw, and finally, there is the skill and vocabulary of the player. Reason and intelligence do matter. Beyond that, you've got some freedom, and you've got some parameters. Just hang in there and play with what other people give you. Go to it!

Reimer shows us it's fun when you're engaged intellectually, and your imagination is piqued through the aesthetic choices he artfully supplies. He's a good read—on personal experience, spirit, gender, Jesus, creation, the fall, salvation, the church, baptism, sexuality, the holy catholic church—that wonderful catechism concept.

And what about personal experience in this engagement with faith? Reimer's helpful cautionary and antidote to faith as narcissistic inwardness: "The challenge is for us to take personal experience seriously without making it the beginning and end of everything. . . . The real question is: Is there something going on in the universe besides our own experience? Are there eternal truths—moral obligations?"

If Reimer had me at "hello," he kept me during his early discussion of "Spirit: The Way to God in Our Technological Way." My own faith pilgrimage attests to the fact that there were days that, without the Spirit ("that which opens up, liberates, embraces the other . . . the opposite of rigidity"), especially those days of my coming of age as a feminist, I would have given up on the church, for sure, and maybe Scripture. Especially for women who sometimes cannot mouth another verse in the male language of God and his Son—there is the Spirit. There is, in Reimer's discussion of the Spirit, nothing particularly new. It is, rather, a review of the Spirit's "remarkable biblical career." And yet, his tender, pure, and clear lyric vision of the Spirit is restorative, and he doesn't see it merely as energy and power, but the Holy Spirit, the bringer, explorer of truth—the liberator.

Reimer's tactic in these essays, wide-ranging references, analogies, and literary choices is embracing of the human spirit: Elie Wiesel, the *Romantische Strasse,* church architecture, Flannery O'Connor, *Schindler's List,* Yasch Siemens or George Brunk, Canadian Jewish minstrel Leonard Cohen, Patrick Friesen's *The Shunning,* The Apostles' Creed, and a host of theologians and political figures from Bonhoeffer and Hitler to Nestor Machno. His inclusiveness damns shortsightedness and a lack of intellectual rigor.

The essays pose intellectual and literary challenges, direct challenges to faith issues, but always imaginatively. "Salvation," for example, that oh-so-loaded term for Mennonites, is not used by Reimer here in a dumbed-down, relativistic sense. He honors the powerful, exciting salvation-bringer, George R. Brunk II: "a larger-than-life figure whose caravan of trucks, massive tent, and powerful rhetoric brought change to traditional Mennonite communal culture." It must have been as exciting as the circus coming to town! One thinks of the pacifist communities that sprang to life with new vigor when the soldiers came through during the Civil War in the U.S., feeling alive for the first time!

Reimer's essays worry that we have lost the thrill, the emotional upsurge and excitement in the faith realm. In fact, if there is a consistent culprit, a consistent antagonist or fall-guy in Reimer's engagement with the great issues of faith, it is *domestication.* Again and again Reimer goes after the human loss of mystery in the engagement with faith issues, the loss of awe in the face of something powerful. He suggests that our hunt has become ordinary, quotidian, mundane, not exciting enough to be attractive or engaging. He wishes we would, with Luther, at least "live boldly that grace may abound"—be engaged enough to require forgiveness and grace, so that we might understand the concepts!

One of my favorite creative writing gurus, Natalie Goldberg, talks about the wild spirit that is the urge toward creation in the written word. It seems to me that *Dogmatic Imagination,* too, would throw off the chains and drudgery of dailiness with regard to faith issues, and wrestle with the angels! Thinking back to his Brunk experience, Reimer laments, "My generation has been so determined not to subject our children to hell fire salvation, that we have domesticated Christianity far too much." He's right. In this age of faith as pabulum, the mush that goes down too easy and has no taste, one relishes this offering which takes as its challenge, not the overthrow of dogma, but the enlivenment of our imaginations concerning those dogmas: "to go deeper by enriching our language."

Raylene Hinz-Penner
Poet and Educator

INTRODUCTION

THEOLOGY IS REFLECTION ON GOD AND ALL THINGS IN relation to God. It is an activity that is not restricted to specialists in the field, but is something that all Christians are called to do. Children, when they ask, "Where did I come from?" and "Where will I go when I die?" are raising questions that are central to theology. Young people who struggle with personal identity, freedom and purpose are dealing with issues at the heart of theology. Everything, from the least important to the most important, visible and invisible, is of theological interest.

What makes something theological is its relation to God. Of course, this begs the ultimate question: "Who or what is God?" This is the first of all theological questions. It is the question that has become especially important in the modern period (eighteenth to twentieth century) when many people have begun wondering whether there even is such a thing as God. Does God really exist? my students ask. When Christians say, "God exists" they are using language in an unusual way. Ordinarily, when we say something exists we are talking about objects in time and space, but God by definition is beyond all time and space. To say God exists would suggest that God is an object beside other objects in time and space, but this is exactly what God is not. God is not an object but a reality beyond all time and space, the ground or source of all objects.

In human experience, "light," "energy" or "love" are perhaps the best examples of realities we believe in that are not objects or spatially restricted. The most consistent biblical descriptions of the mystery called God are that "God is Spirit" and "God is Love." We see in these terms how the very essence of God (Spirit) in the Bible is connected with relationship and ethics (Love). This direct connection between "who God is" and "how we ought to relate to others" has been especially important for Mennonites.

The theological reflections included in this volume are meant to be easily accessible meditations on core Christian beliefs, sometimes referred to as "doctrines" (or teachings): the Bible, God, Christ, Spirit, creation, salvation, the church, love, hell, heaven, the end of time and history. The title, "The Dogmatic Imagination," is intended to counter the common misconception that confessions, doctrines, dogmas and creeds (a family of terms all related to "right thinking" about faith) necessarily mean rigidity, inflexibility, and intolerance, as in the words "doctrinaire" or "dogmatism." In the early Christian period, doctrines, creeds and dogmas were thought of as symbols of faith that developed over time. They were dynamic, which is why I have subtitled this volume, "The Dynamics of Christian Belief."

I use the metaphor of the Scrabble game to convey this sense of dynamism. Frequent allusions to literature (fiction and poetry), painting, music, architecture, and other forms of art remind us that in using theological language we enter the world of the imagination. Theological language, in seeking to open up spiritual, non–empirical dimensions of existence, is dependent on diverse forms of speech and communication: simile, metaphor, analogy, parable, myth, saga, sign, symbol, paradox, and dialectic. Modern linguistic theory talks about "speech acts," the power of language to make things happen. A curse or a blessing, for example, does not merely describe something but is an act which creates its own reality. All of these different ways of speaking are found in the Bible.

The ancients (classical and medieval theologians) interpreted biblical texts in four ways: literal (not to be confused with literalistic, but meaning a straight-forward reading), allegorical (a spiritual or mystical reading), tropological (a moral and ethical reading), and anagogical (a futuristic reading). It is important when reading the Bible and thinking theologically to remember that theology is a specific way of speaking about reality that uses language differently than disciplines dealing with biology and matter.

These essays are meant to inspire readers to catch the excitement of thinking theologically about the awesome and extraordinary as well as the mundane dimensions of life. Above all, I hope to convey the sense that theological reflection is a dynamic and imaginative way of looking at the world, one which is never closed or finished.

A. James Reimer
February 2003

ACKNOWLEDGMENTS

MOST OF THE ESSAYS IN THIS VOLUME APPEARED PREVIOUSLY in a series called "Dynamics of Belief," published over a two-year period (1993–1995) in the *Mennonite Reporter,* since then renamed *Canadian Mennonite.* Some of the essays have been slightly modified. Three additional meditations appear at the end of the volume, two of them previously unpublished.

I thank Mennonite Publishing Service for the permission to reprint the articles here, and Margaret Loewen Reimer for applying her editorial skills to the copy. I am indebted to Levi Miller of Herald Press for his encouragement to submit these essays for publication. I also want to acknowledge the inspiration I have received from my students over many years of teaching.

FAITH

A Jigsaw Puzzle or a Scrabble Game?

I N 1958, WHEN I WAS SIXTEEN YEARS OLD, I WAS BAP-
tized into the Bergthaler Mennonite Church in Manitoba. In preparation, we baptismal candidates were taken
through a little blue book called *Catechism*. This book con-
sisted of some 200 questions and answers—German on one
side and English on the other—concerning what we as
Mennonite Christians believe about God, creation, human
nature, sin and the Fall, salvation, the Christian life, and the
end of time and history.

Every year, between New Year's and Pentecost, young
people who wanted to be baptized were taken through these
beliefs. And every year, the whole congregation listened to
the candidates (sitting in the front pews) give their answers
to these questions and to the preacher preach on the questions of that day. As a result, all the members of the church
were given a yearly review of the whole Christian story, and
preachers had to discipline themselves to preach on given
topics. This was the closest that Mennonites came to following a lectionary and to systematic theological thinking.

Some Mennonite groups, of course, never had such a
practice. And in the 1960s, those that did dropped it in favor

of small, intimate discussion sessions with pastors and those interested in joining the church. The old way was perceived to be dull and impersonal. But the shift in style also changed the way we talk about Mennonite faith. Earlier, there was an emphasis on objective doctrines and beliefs; this gave way to an increasing focus on personal relationships, feelings, and social action. This new approach had a great deal of positive value as it connected belief to real life and human experience.

Unfortunately, however, people tended to forget the basic categories of belief, and children never learned them. From my experience, the older generation knows and loves the language of doctrine, the middle generation (my age) remembers it but does not like it, and my children's generation does not know it.

But my experience has also convinced me that people want to know Christianity's basic beliefs. Teaching first-year theology students at university, baptismal candidates at church, and talking to my own children have revealed that young people are eager to be inspired by the language of belief. I find that children and youth are interested in the big questions of meaning—questions about how the parts fit into a whole.

We cannot go back to the past. The challenge is to embrace the world in which we live, but through the eyes of traditional wisdom: to capture the imagination of our young people through their natural inclinations toward the supernatural, the magical, the fantastical, and the innovative.

When my son was thirteen years old he made the comment: "If only I could see a ghost, just once, even if it would kill me. Then at least I would know there is such a thing."

His comment reflects the inclinations of his generation. There is a kind of gloom, a sense of hopelessness about the future of this planet that hovers over young people. They have a vague foreboding that because of what we are doing to our environment and to each other, things are grinding to a halt. If there were such a ghostly, supernatural realm, beyond the material, physical world, then there might be some hope. This is where the eternal truths of the Christian faith come in.

The challenge for us is to take basic beliefs (doctrines) of the historic Christian faith and, together with our youth, re-imagine their meaning for today. There is a dynamic quality to these beliefs that stands the test of time and change, an inner structure that is more like a Scrabble game than a jigsaw puzzle.

Take the jigsaw puzzle. The whole game is predetermined; there is virtually no freedom. The picture is fixed. There is a specific number of pieces and each piece fits only one spot. The point of the puzzle is to discover where a particular piece fits to make the picture come out right. You may start at different places, but in the end it makes no difference—the outcome is fixed.

A variety of factors determines the outcome of a Scrabble game. First, there is a fixed component. The game board has a limited number of squares and there is an unalterable alphabet with predetermined values for each letter. Second, people have to respect the rules of the game. Each person is allowed a certain number of letters, must take turns, and place words in a certain way on the board. Third, there is a matter of luck in picking letters and getting good opportunities for words. Fourth, there is the skill and vocabulary of the player. Reason and intelligence are also involved in Scrabble.

Within the limits and rules of the game, however, there is virtually unlimited freedom. No two games are ever the same. The final shape of the game is clear only at the end. The most important point is that players play the game and hang in there until the end. The design (meaning, you might say) emerges with the playing. Further, each person's success depends on the moves of other people playing. It is a game in which players are dependent on each other while remaining free and independent.

Faith and beliefs, I propose, are more like the dynamics of a Scrabble game than the rules of a jigsaw puzzle. In this book I want to look at the central beliefs of the Christian faith, using the metaphor of the Scrabble game. However, I don't want to disregard the truth of the jigsaw puzzle as a metaphor altogether. There is a predetermined structure, which might be referred to as "laws of nature," which we disregard at our own peril. The cosmos is not entirely open.

2

THE BIBLE
Fact or Fiction?

S OME YEARS AGO, I ASKED MY UNDERGRADUATE CLASS to read the book *Night,* Elie Wiesel's account of his horrific experiences as a Jewish teenager in Auschwitz, the Nazi death camp. Wiesel happened to be giving a lecture at a neighboring university and I took the class to hear him.

It was an astonishing experience! Wiesel, who a year later received the Nobel Prize for literature, kept a large audience of university students and professors spellbound with his imaginative reading of the Genesis story of Noah, the flood, and the rainbow.

Wiesel wrestled with the biblical text, in particular God's promise never to destroy the world again. We were in the heat of the Cold War years and it was a comfort to think that our fears of imminent nuclear disaster were unfounded. A reread, however, robbed Wiesel of all such easy security. God had promised never again to destroy the world by flood, but no assurances against nuclear fire. A third reading made things worse: what if we ourselves, not God, annihilate the world?

This is the way the Bible ought to be wrestled with. The text as the vehicle for divine truths is the point of reference. The particular situations in which we find ourselves drive us back to God and the text again and again. But it's not an easy read. There are no quick solutions. No avoiding the texts that don't seem to suit our experience, yet no deifying of the text, either. The process of determining God's word for us, the readers, is dynamic, full of uncomfortable surprises, and never devoid of human responsibility.

I've been catching up on Mennonite literature lately and have been impressed by its theological relevance. Many writers offer us a language beyond the literalistic and the prosaic. It is a language that is often closer to real life experience than church talk is. It is the language of poetry, story, parable, metaphor, and analogy.

This language is commonly referred to as fiction. Ironically, so-called "fiction" is often truer to life than "nonfiction." One writer says that stories "lead one back into the passionate, sad, exhilarating experiences of real life," while "dogmas lead to nowhere but valleys of dry bones."

The challenge is not to throw out dogmas (teachings) of the church, but to enliven our imagination concerning them—to go deeper by enriching our language. American novelist Flannery O'Connor claimed that it is precisely the church's formulations of faith that help us to penetrate reality. "Christian dogma is about the only thing left in the world that surely guards and respects mystery," she said.

I remember first setting foot in a graduate theology class at the University of Toronto. I had come from years of studying philosophy and history, deeply entrenched in a kind of philosophical skepticism and historical literalism. I was dumbfounded by what I heard: an unapologetic defense of traditional dogmas of the Christian faith. I was tempted to go back to studying history.

It took me a while to understand that these dogmas (traditional formulations of Christian beliefs) were expressed in theological language, a language very different from scientific and empirical language. It is a way of speaking about the deepest dimensions of human existence; it presupposes a spiritual reality behind ordinary life and experience. It was a language I had grown up with but had virtually forgotten.

Theological language has much in common with literary ways of speaking. It is the rich and multidimensional language of the imagination, the language of transparency. It is the language of the Bible.

I know people with little education who know much of the Bible "by heart" (an expression suggesting deeper than intellectual knowledge) and who read lengthy passages at one sitting. They read the Bible literally but with a lively imagination, making big leaps back and forth between parts of the Bible and between past and present. I sometimes wonder whether their intuitive reading may not yield a better understanding of what is going on with God, the text, and human beings than many a scholar who labors over word and text with all the resources of learning.

The Bible uses many different genres and languages (stories, parables, sayings, songs, letters, confessions, visions, dreams) to express the encounter with the divine in the midst of life. Early Christians believed that the Bible had both literal and hidden/cosmic meanings. The literal was the straightforward meaning (e.g. the Song of Solomon is actual love poetry between two people). Yet a literal reading was not a literalistic reading in which every word had a rigid, fixed meaning. The ancients did not read the Bible literalistically.

In addition to the literal, they found hidden meanings in the text. For example, the Song of Solomon describes the soul's relation to God (a tropological/moral reading) or Christ's relation to the church (an allegorical reading). Ideally, primacy was given to the straightforward reading, but the imagination was encouraged to play with hidden meanings.

This is something like the music of J. S. Bach. The bass line (continuo) firmly grounds the piece while the instruments dance around on the top, giving the music its lively interest. The continuo in the Scriptures is the Christian belief that God speaks to us through these texts in a unique, authoritative, and dynamic way. To go back to the game analogy in chapter 1, the Scrabble game, even though it involves many variables, presupposes design and purpose. In the same way, the Christian assumes the existence of cosmic meaning. In the biblical text, the human word becomes the medium for the eternal word, and the eternal word constantly takes on human meaning. (The late choral director Robert Shaw suggested another dynamic of that idea when he said that in the creative act, the flesh becomes word.)

Eternal word becoming flesh and flesh becoming word—the biblical text is an interplay between these two movements. This divine weaving together of many truths and ways of speaking will be completed only at the end of time.

3

EXPERIENCE
No Other Foundation?

F LORENCE, ITALY, IS HOME TO SOME OF THE GREAT marble sculptures of Michelangelo (1475–1564). One of the most famous is the almost perfect "David." His later, roughly hewn and unfinished sculptures, however, are much more interesting. My favorite is called "Awakening Captive." It shows a human figure in the process of emerging out of a mass of stone. The dynamic, sensual male figure is struggling to free himself from undifferentiated rock.

Michelangelo's sculpture represents, we might say, the birth of the experiencing and thinking individual subject, the struggle of the individual for liberation from mass humanity and external authorities such as tradition, church, dogma, and king. This emancipation of the individual human being from all forms of constraint characterizes much of the modern vision. We know that there are negative consequences of this vision of unlimited human freedom, especially in modern science and technology. But there are also positive aspects.

Take the women's movement. The male figure in the sculpture might just as well have been a female figure struggling to free herself from patriarchal captivity. Feminists have made a point of stressing individual experience (particularly women's experience) as a crucial factor in interpreting the Bible and reimagining Christian faith. The challenge is for us to take personal experience seriously without making it the beginning and end of everything.

It is a misunderstanding to pit experience against the Bible or tradition, as though the latter two are somehow outside of the former. The Bible and tradition are the cumulative experience of the ages and the collective reflection upon that experience. One might even say that the Bible is a product of Jewish and early Christian tradition and experience. Women rightly remind us that women's experiences have too often been disregarded in this library of experience.

But the real question is: Is there something going on in the universe besides our own experience? Is God addressing us? Is there a breaking into our experience from beyond? Are there eternal truths—moral obligations? If so, our personal experience cannot be the foundation upon which all else is built. Our experience then is more like a response to that which is going on already.

Furthermore, there is a long tradition of human experience and wisdom within which our own experience of liberation takes on meaning. Isolated from that larger tradition, and our smaller communal traditions, our individual freedom is empty and meaningless.

This sense of a living community of experience is perhaps no more movingly portrayed than in the Hebrew Scriptures. Here we have memories of deliverance, miraculous interventions, divine commands, humiliating defeats and great victories, flawed leaders and rebellious followers, hierarchy and protest, and the ordinary, everyday struggle to survive.

In Deuteronomy 6 we have a Scrabble-game-like interplay of four components of Hebrew faith that are highly instructive for us even today:

1. There are the eternal truths—commandments, statutes, and ordinances.

2. There is the responsibility of passing on the tradition to the children through daily storytelling.

3. There is the content of what is to be passed on—the promises of God to our ancestors, the experiences of previous generations, and the divine truths.

4. Most important, there is a call for a particular kind of experience—a personal relationship with God. "You shall love the Lord your God with all your heart, and with all your soul, and with all your might."

At the foundation of the commandments and of tradition is experience, but it is not the experience of the autonomous self pursuing individual rights (self-love). It is rather the experience of being grasped by a love for God who is both distant from us and closer to us than we are to ourselves, and in whom (to use Pauline language) we live and move and have our being.

4

SPIRIT

The Way to God in Our Technological Age

I HAVE OFTEN WONDERED WHY THREE OF MY STEIN-bach, Manitoba, aunts left the *Kleinegemeinde* Mennonites to join the Pentecostals. The *Kleinegemeinde* (meaning "small church"), a breakaway from the main Mennonite church in Russia, was founded by my ancestor, Klaas Reimer. What did the Pentecostals have over the Mennonites? Did they have more spiritual dynamism? Was there more room for women?

All I know is that the debate over whether one had the gift of the Holy Spirit or not (usually framed in terms of "speaking in tongues") produced considerable tension within the extended Reimer family. What a strange fruit of the Spirit! This was my first introduction to the doctrine of the Holy Spirit.

Each age has its own religious preoccupations. People in the late Middle Ages, for example, were preoccupied with sin, penance, pilgrimages, and salvation. Luther's message of justification through faith alone, and not by human merit, immediately caught the imagination of the people. The modern age, as no age before it, has been bedeviled by the problem of God.

The very existence of a God beyond ourselves, who makes the world (creation), takes care of it (preservation), and guides it toward a goal (providence), has become a problem. Many people either deliberately or through indifference no longer take seriously such a divine reality.

Technology (the art of making), the most important fact of modern existence, presupposes that human beings are free to shape the world without interference by reference to a divine reality. We are the ones who make! The word "technology" combines two Latin terms: *techne* (making) and *logos* (thinking), thus creating a new concept in the modern period. Thinking is identified with making, quite different from the older understanding of reason as contemplation. Technology is not just hardware, such as machines or computers, but is a way of thinking about reality in terms of usefulness and efficiency.

Prayer, for example, can become "technique" rather than contemplation. The songs we sing, the prayers we pray, and the sermons we hear on Sunday morning are frequently little more than attempts to manipulate God for our own purposes. This has the effect of making the divine mystery of God irrelevant to the way we view the world and make decisions.

Ironically, it is precisely now, when God seems most irrelevant, that the question of divine transcendence is most urgent. But how is such divine reality to be imagined? As Spirit! That which is both nearest to our spirit and yet unlike anything else we know. That which, like love, is within the realm of ordinary experience, yet without boundaries, beyond space and time. No one, not even the church, has a monopoly on it.

Spirit is that which opens up, liberates, embraces the other. Spirit is the opposite of rigidity—it errs on the side of generosity and may lead to ecstasy (standing outside oneself). It is frequently unconventional. It may fragment on one level, but on the deepest level it unites.

Technology treats nature, the world, and human beings as dead stuff at our disposal, as means to our own "progressive" ends. Spirit, on the contrary, is the breath of God that raises the dead to life: "The Lord God formed man from the dust of the ground, and breathed into his nostrils the breath of life" (Genesis 2:7). Our own life is the very breath of God.

The biblical career of the Spirit is a most remarkable one. At the creation of the world, the Spirit of God moved over the waters, helping to create order out of chaos. The Spirit gave life to the first human beings. The Spirit set Ezekiel down in the valley of dry bones and gave life to those bones. The prophet Joel announced that the Spirit would be poured out on all people (sons and daughters, male servants and female servants) on the day of the Lord.

The Spirit played an indispensable role in the conception of Jesus. The Spirit descended upon Jesus at his baptism and led him into the desert to be tempted. Jesus' ministry of teaching and healing was made possible through the Spirit. The Spirit was before, in, and after Jesus.

Jesus promised that the Spirit would come to his disciples after he was gone. Jesus was raised from the dead by the Spirit—the same Spirit that raises us from the dead now and in the age to come. It is the Spirit that came to all the believers at Pentecost and gave birth to the church. The Spirit drove the first missionary movement as reported in the book of Acts. It is the Spirit that has been present with the church throughout the ages and has given rise again and again to renewal movements within the church, movements in which women frequently play leading roles.

It is the Spirit that showed John the great vision of the Apocalypse. The Spirit was present at the origin of this world and the birth of the new one.

We usually think of the Spirit primarily as energy, power, and giver of life. In the Bible, however, the Spirit is also referred to as the Spirit of truth. As the church faces urgent moral and ethical dilemmas (e.g. reproductive technologies, homosexuality, euthanasia) that are not easily addressed by quoting Bible verses, we need this Spirit of insight and wisdom to make decisions and move forward.

The Spirit that Christ promises frees us to explore new possibilities. This is why Jesus said that his departure would be fortunate for his disciples. After he left they would receive the Spirit of truth which would reveal to them things they were not yet ready to hear from him (John 16:12-13). In fact, they would do greater works than Jesus himself had done (John 14:12).

This is not just any spirit. It is not simply a "world spirit" or "human spirit" or "mother earth spirit." It is Holy Spirit, identifiable by its gifts (1 Corinthians 12:4-11) and fruits (Galatians 5:22-23). It is none other than the Spirit of Christ and of God present to the whole world.

5

GOD THE FATHER
He or She?

N THE SPRING OF 1992, MY SON AND I TRAVELED along the *Romantische Strasse* (Romantic Road) in Germany. It begins in Würzburg and ends in Füssen, home of *Neuschwanstein,* the famous castle of the "mad" King Ludwig. This beautiful road is known for its many baroque churches, such as the ones in Rothenburg and Wies.

Architecture is one indicator of the beliefs of an age, and these churches of the seventeenth and eighteenth centuries, with their lavish ornamentation, reflect an era that was increasingly preoccupied with this world. In fact, I realized how the changing style of churches throughout history reveals a changing concept of God and how we worship God.

In the high Middle Ages, the fortress-like Romanesque churches with their heavy round arches convey a sense of security, permanence, and unshakable faith. The massive stone walls leave no doubt that the church believed it possessed the eternal truth of God, both dogmatically and institutionally.

With the Renaissance, Reformation, and the early modern period came Gothic architecture. This is the style I prefer—simple, slender, vertical lines leading the human imagination upward into the beyond. The roof is held up elegantly with membrane-like, ribbed vaulting. As one enters a Gothic church, one immediately has the sense of great height, suggesting infinite space and transcendence, with light radiating through stained-glass windows. This is an age no longer as willing to take dogmatic permanence for granted. It is an age of new openness.

The later baroque churches tend to be lower, fancier, and more self-indulgent, particularly evident in the gaudy decoration of the rococo style. One has the sense that the lavish paintings of divine realms on the ceilings are but fanciful projections of the mind, and that faith remains trapped within the human sphere.

Mennonites have always prided themselves on the plainness of their church buildings, partly out of necessity (to escape detection in the early years), but also for theological reasons. Simple buildings emphasize a simple style of life and worship, and the importance of human relationships. Some of us even worship in low-ceilinged, multipurpose rooms. What kind of imagining about God does this inspire? How does our society, largely defined by consumerism, self-indulgence, and political correctness, think about God?

We are not a secular society. Opinion polls show that a large percentage of North Americans not only believe in God, but identify themselves as Christian. What God is this that so many of us believe in?

If there is one overriding affirmation about God in the Hebrew Scriptures it is that Yahweh is beyond all human imagination, understanding, and form. Listen to Moses: "Take care and watch yourselves closely, so that you do not act corruptly by making an idol for yourselves, in the form of any figure—the likeness of male or female" (Deuteron-omy 4:16).

Again and again in the Bible, God is portrayed not as an object in the usual sense, but as a subject (an "I") that addresses people from the beyond, frequently in the most unexpected situations. "Then the Lord spoke to you out of the fire. You heard the sound of words, but saw no form; there was only a voice" (Deuteronomy 4:12). This is the mystery: God is beyond space and time, neither male nor female, and yet God speaks and acts personally, and expects a personal response.

Some of the most intense debates in the committee that prepared the most recent Mennonite hymnal *(Hymnal: A Worship Book)* occurred over what language to use for God. One criterion was to use inclusive language wherever pos-sible, another to include texts with a variety of metaphors for God. For example, one new hymn is "Mothering God, you gave me birth." No one can deny the predominance of male imagery for God in the Bible. We are also aware, how-ever, of the feminine images such as "I will cry out like a woman in labor" (Isaiah 42:14) or "You forgot the God who gave you birth" (Deuteronomy 32:18).

And isn't it interesting how Genesis alludes to the image of God in the creation story? "So God created humankind in his image, in the image of God he created them; male and female he created them" (1:27). The ancient writers knew full well that God was neither male nor female, but beyond all human form. These images were but ways of talking about a personal, caring, judging God.

Israel emphasized the maleness of God to distinguish its faith from the nature religions in surrounding cultures. To the Hebrews, maleness represented transcendence (otherness) while femaleness represented immanence (nearness).

Symbols such as these have great emotional and religious power, a power that develops over long periods of time. That is why people feel so strongly about traditional images for God and why they cannot be readily replaced. Nevertheless, symbols and their meanings do change, including symbols of masculinity and femininity. They sometimes lose their power and gradually are replaced over time.

The issue is not whether God is male or female—we know God is neither. What is at stake is God's otherness. This is particularly important in our age of environmental concerns that is prone to think of God as near to nature ("nature friendly"). The Holy Spirit (the third way of God's being) is God near us and within us (see chapter 4). God's first way of being, traditionally referred to as God the Father, is God's mysterious otherness (divine creator of the world). The challenge is to find images that best capture this mystery of God in our time.

6

JESUS-CHRIST
A Composite Drawing

A N OLDER PERSON RECENTLY SAID TO ME RUEFULLY, "IT seems to me everybody's talking about God these days, but no one is talking about Jesus anymore."

Interestingly, Mennonites have tended to speak more about Jesus than God. This begs the question: What is Jesus' relationship to God? The oft-quoted verse, "I am the way, and the truth, and the life. No one comes to the Father except through me" (John 14:6), begs the same question. This verse is frequently drawn upon in heated debates about the exclusive claims of Jesus in relation to other religions, but leaves us wondering: which Jesus?

The Bible gives us many pictures of Jesus: Jesus as the Logos (John 1), Jesus as servant (Philippians 2:5–7), Jesus as adopted son (Matthew 3:17), Jesus as example (Hebrew 12), Jesus as exclusive way (John 14:6), Jesus as the inclusive one (Ephesians 1:10), Jesus as God (John 20:28). These are only a few of the many biblical pictures of Jesus and do not include the numerous honorary titles: Christ, Son of God, Son of Man, Messiah, Lord.

Jesus himself was modest about his role and identity, and told people not to tell others about him being the Christ.

This is sometimes referred to as the "messianic secret." One time he even said, "Why do you call me good? No one is good but God alone" (Mark 10:18). This is quite the opposite of my son's impression when he was young. "I don't like Jesus," he said. Why? "Because he's too arrogant. He thought he was God." Even though Jesus claimed unity and oneness with God, he never equated himself with the Father.

Is there then no underlying unity that draws all these pictures of Jesus together? This is precisely the question the early church asked. Who is this Jesus whom we worship? What the church of the first few centuries did was make a composite drawing of Jesus, particularly in relation to God and the Spirit. We know about composite sketches from "Wanted!" posters in which police imagine what the criminal looks like on the basis of sightings and clues. The early church, however, was not only concerned with getting back to the original Jesus, but with how Jesus was being experienced in an ongoing way, how he was being worshiped, and how he was being distorted.

In other words, it was the integrity of the living Jesus with which they were primarily concerned. It was not only the Jesus of Nazareth but Jesus-Christ (Christ is not a surname but an honorary title, thus the hyphenation) they wanted to preserve against heresy.

We do not like the term "heresy." It sounds too judgmental. Maybe it's because we misunderstand it. We tend to think of it as meaning too broad or liberal a view. Actually, heresy means too narrow a view. It is taking one of the many pictures of Jesus-Christ, the one that suits us best, and making it the only one, taking one piece of the pie and assuming it to be the whole.

The early church's composite drawing of Jesus-Christ within the Christian triune doctrine of God was an attempt to be as embracing and comprehensive as possible, to include both the plurality and the singularity of God, to guard against narrowing.

According to a recent television biography, former Prime Minister of Canada Pierre Trudeau, as a young Catholic taking catechism, once beat up another boy for denying the Trinity. As a young Mennonite, I might have been the recipient of his blows. Mennonites have been a bit shy about the doctrine of the Trinity. Nevertheless, it is at the very heart of the Christian understanding of God, distinguishing it from other religions.

Underlying the historical development of the doctrine of the Trinity are three convictions:

1. As Jews, the first Christians believed in the one and only transcendent God of the Jews (Yahweh).

2. As those who had experienced Jesus-Christ personally (the forgiveness of sin, the resurrected life), they believed they had experienced the one God of the Jews in Jesus.

3. As believers filled with the Holy Spirit at Pentecost, these early Christians were convinced that they were experiencing the very Spirit of Yahweh and Jesus-Christ.

The early Christians began talking of the one God in three ways: as the Father (transcendent mystery and creator of the world), as Spirit (dynamic inner power source of ongoing insight and spiritual motor of the church), and as Son (specific, historical person-event).

Metaphors that might help us visualize this come from the world of music. Is God like a conductor or is God like a concertmaster? As a conductor, God is separate, in control, directing. As a concertmaster, God is one of the players yet different, subtly holding things together through solidarity, tuning, indirect inspiration, and influence. God is really both. There is a sense in which God is the distant, mysterious conductor of the whole symphony. But there is also a sense in which God is close and one of us (inner Spirit), a concertmaster.

What about the other component—Christ? A student of mine suggested expanding the above analogy. One might say Christ is the composition. In Jesus-Christ's birth, life, teaching, death, and resurrection we have the score or the script, the specific content of what we believe. So God is all three: conductor ("Father"), concertmaster (Spirit) and composition (Son).

7

CREATION
Back to the Future

W HAT I LIKE MOST ABOUT DREAMS AND VISIONS IS THAT they do not obey the ordinary rules of time and space. They have no particular order and no apparent regard for seconds, minutes, hours, days, years, centuries, millennia. In a few dream-moments we can experience a lifetime. We change into other beings or become disembodied. We find ourselves living in other eras. In a dream, the future might as well be past, the past future, down up, and up down. Time stands still, is interrupted, or reversed. Anything is possible.

Current scientific theories of relativity, the curvature of space and time, the interchangeability of energy and matter—popularized in science fiction and futuristic movies— add nothing new to the world of dreams.

The Bible is full of such dreams and visions—the metamorphosis of spirit into matter, matter into spirit, the suspension of time. One of the most fascinating is John's vision of the end of the world and the beginning of a new one in the book of Revelation. I have often thought that if John's vision of "a new heaven and new earth," of "the holy city, the new Jerusalem, coming down out of heaven from God" is a vision or prophecy of the future, then Genesis 1 and 2 is a kind of backward prophecy, a vision of the past.

The creation story is a vision of what the world was in its perfect, original state, and of what it might once again become. Revelation becomes Genesis and Genesis becomes Revelation. The future comes to be out of the original biblical vision in strange, unexpected ways. What is the Christian vision of creation? It has to do with how we see the world and our place in it, how we view nature and our relation to it.

Genesis, probably compiled between 900 and 400 B.C.E., is not essentially concerned with scientific explanations, such as the Big Bang Theory of the origin of the universe fifteen billion years ago, or evolutionary theories of the development of life, or the most recent views of quantum mechanics or molecular biology.

Why is there anything at all? What kind of beings are we? Are we gods or gardeners? These are the basic questions behind the creation vision at the beginning of the Bible. These are theological questions rather than scientific ones (although they have implications for each other).

The first creation vision (Genesis 1:1–2:4a) has a well-ordered symmetry to it, with human beings coming as the climax of creation. God says (note the plural): "Let us make humankind in our image, according to our likeness." Human beings are given the task of filling the earth, subduing it, and having dominion over all living things (sometimes called the "cultural mandate").

The second creation story (Genesis 2:4b–25) is much less systematic and ordered, with a rather different vision of humanity. Human beings are created at the very beginning from the ground and given life by the breath (spirit) of God. We are physically tied to nature (our finitude) and spiritually linked to God, free from nature (our infinitude). The cultural mandate in this second account is much softer: to till and keep the garden, as deputies of the divine.

Here we have two visions of our role in the cosmos. Too often we have taken the first vision as justifying our dream of becoming gods—conquering, ruling, and having dominion over each other and the earth, thereby destroying all (the Fall). Too often we lose sight of the second vision—gardening, tilling, and taking care of the world. (A former student of mine goes so far as to practice nonviolent gardening, using no sharp instruments to break the soil.)

Creation is always dynamic, always changing. It is ongoing. The apostle Paul gives us a fascinating image of the whole creation yearning for the kind of freedom given human beings: "For the creation waits with eager longing for the revealing of the children of God . . . that the creation itself will be set free from its bondage to decay and will obtain the freedom of the glory of the children of God" (Romans 8:19-21).

Nature is waiting for the "children of God" who themselves have been liberated by the Son of God. What an interesting thought! The redemption of nature is dependent on human redemption, for human beings to be freed from self-interest to become responsible agents in the world as God intended in the Garden of Eden. The Son is "the firstborn of all creation; for in him all things in heaven and on earth were created, things visible and invisible" (Colossians 1:15-16). "So if anyone is in Christ, there is a new creation: everything old has passed away, see, everything has become new!" (2 Corinthians 5:17).

What role are we to play in this liberation of creation? This redemption begins in small ways. Remember the movie, *Schindler's List,* in which a not altogether virtuous man transcended himself by buying the lives of some 1,100 Jews from Auschwitz to work in his factory. At the end, realizing he could have saved even more lives by melting down his gold Nazi pin, he is overcome by remorse. His Jewish accountant reassures him with an old Jewish proverb: "By saving one person you have redeemed the world."

8

THE FALL
Knowing Good and Evil

O NE OF MY THEOLOGY PROFESSORS ONCE TOLD ME: "Reimer, the problem with you is your Mennonite moralism. You need to think of the worst sin you could commit, then go and do it. After that you would either not be able to live with yourself, or you would learn to live by the grace of God."

I wouldn't recommend this course of action to anyone, but he did have a point: Our self-perceptions about how good we are, or how good our church is, frequently prevent us from doing the truly good. The truly good is the genuine love of God and others. Sin is the distorted love of self or self-preoccupation—using nature, things, people, or God for one's own aggrandizement—frequently disguised as love for others.

Another name for this is self-righteousness, cloaking our inner insecurities with nice external behavior in order to make a good impression, thereby making us feel that we are better than others.

Sometimes our poets, novelists, and journalists do a better job than others of exposing the dark and abusive underside of ourselves and our churches, not sparing even the official

gatekeepers of the tradition. I am fascinated by the phenom-
enon of the good-for-nothing who does something truly
good in spite of himself. The main character (played by
Dustin Hoffman) in the movie *Hero* is in many ways a despi-
cable person (he does not play by the normal rules of family
and moral expectations). Yet because he happens to be at a
certain place at a certain time, he saves a whole planeload of
doomed people, against all his own instincts.

We are really all in the same boat. Our natural instincts
are for self-preservation even at the expense of others. This
is our fallen nature, our original sin. We live in a sinful world.
The damage done to nature in the name of progress, the
atrocities committed in the name of our nation, and the barbarism ordinary good people are capable of when circumstances are right are all reflections of what we are all capable.

This truth has been forcefully brought home to me by
our "Yugoslav" friends. In the early 1990s, we played a small
part in helping a family of four—a Serbian father, Croatian
mother, and two small children—emigrate to Canada from
the former Yugoslavia. They had seen how it is that good,
loving people in times of crisis can become vicious and
cruel.

Who knows what demons lurk in our subconscious? Job,
the Psalmist, Paul, St. Augustine, and Luther knew all about
this long before Freud. The author of Genesis too had
remarkable insight into the fallen nature of the world. In
the creation accounts, human beings are given special status
(created in the likeness of God) with special responsibility
to take care of the world. But boundaries are put around
this responsibility; the tree of life and the tree of good and
evil are off limits.

This second tree is of special interest. Why were Adam and Eve not to eat of it? The serpent (interesting that an animal is the smartest of all and the source of temptation) argues that God knows human beings will become like God, knowing good and evil, if they eat of this tree. When they do eat, they lose their innocence—their eyes are opened and they hide from each other (by covering themselves) and from God (out of fear).

Wherein lies the evil? Is it not precisely the misuse of a good thing—their freedom, their image-of-godness? The reason why sin and evil are so seductive is because they are the perversion of the good. Our very goodness can be the source of evil.

The punishment meted out by God (another way of talking about the consequence of the fall) is also fascinating. For the first time, there will be hostility between humans and the animal kingdom ("I will put enmity between you [the serpent] and the woman, and between your offspring and hers"), domination of male over female ("he shall rule over you"), alienation of humanity and nature ("thorns and thistles it shall bring forth for you"), the corruption of nature ("cursed is the ground because of you"), and death itself ("to dust you shall return").

The writers of Genesis saw all of creation as interconnected. When humanity presupposed unlimited freedom, the result was domination, alienation, and loss of the connections—estrangement on all levels. They lost the garden.

We are told that God sent Adam and Eve out of the garden to prevent them from eating of the first tree (the tree of life) and thus living forever (Genesis 3:22–23). This tree of life later became an important symbol, identified with Jesus.

As the Bible begins, so it ends, with the tree of life. What is new is that now the tree of life is in the midst of the city. In John's Apocalypse we have the following vision: "Then the angel showed me the river of the water of life, bright as crystal, flowing from the throne of God. . . . On either side of the river, is the tree of life with its twelve kinds of fruit . . . and the leaves of the tree are for the healing of the nations" (Revelation 22:1–2).

This is a vision of reconnection, of the reunification of the world. The tree of life in the Garden of Eden is the sign of divine grace (life) that is present from the beginning. This tree of grace is at the heart of creation. God's prohibition against eating from this tree of life indicates that grace is not ours for the taking; it is a gift offered to us at God's initiative.

9

PRESERVATION
Does God Play Dice with the World?

A LBERT EINSTEIN WAS MORE THAN A PHYSICIST. HE WAS a philosopher wondering about the big questions—how did the universe come to be? What makes it tick? After his armchair discovery of relativity theory and the interchangeability of energy and matter ($E=MC^2$), he began a lifelong search for a unified theory—a simple key to everything there is. This quest for the Holy Grail of the cosmos continues with Cambridge physicist Stephen Hawking.

Theology (faith seeking understanding) and philosophy (love of wisdom) were historically almost indistinguishable. In the past two centuries, not only have they been separated, most often they have forgotten their vocation, which is to meditate on the whole, on the connections of things.

Einstein speculated about whether God plays dice with the world. Is there a fundamental coherence to all reality, he wondered, or is the world capricious, governed by chance? Many contemporary thinkers claim that what we see is what we get: disconnectedness, fragmentation, and lack of cohesion at the deepest level. It is a tempting conclusion in the light of Bosnia, Rwanda, and September 11.

The ancients presupposed an eternal order (logos). They saw time as "the moving shadow of eternity," as the Canadian philosopher George Grant put it. Time, history, and human behavior were measured by an external standard: God's eternal will and being.

Moderns have reversed this. Eternity has come to be the fleeting shadow of time, the projection of human wishes and imagination. Time, progress, movement from past to present to future, and forward direction are everything. Some modern philosophers, such as Friedrich Nietzsche, have called this the loss of all horizons, the "death of God." We are on an open sea without a shoreline by which to locate ourselves.

This has profound implications for our behavior (ethics). If there is no marker to determine where we stand, no eternal measure, then morality becomes a matter of human values determined by those in power, or, to use Nietzsche's language, it is the "will to power."

The modern theory of relativity has sometimes been used to bolster this belief in the total relativity of all things, including morality. But it is interesting that for Einstein there was a constant—the speed of light—by which all things could be judged. The sciences, especially pure mathematics, continue to presuppose formulas and equations (like Plato's ideal forms) by which to understand reality.

This brings me to the Christian doctrine of preservation and providence, traditionally considered sub-doctrines of creation. Preservation has to do with God's preserving or keeping of the world. Providence deals with God's leading or bringing the world to its final end or purpose. The question is: How is God's preservation of the world mediated (what means does God use)?

I believe, with Einstein, that the universe is not fundamentally capricious, incoherent, totally open-ended. I believe that behind or beneath the apparent disconnectedness and fragmentation there is an order, a structure within which history and our actions take on their meaning and obligations. These structures (one might cautiously call them "laws") play a part in God's preservation of the world. God's will is not purely arbitrary, but is at least partly mediated through rules, orders, ordinances, and institutions not solely of human construction.

How human institutions—family, nation and state, society and culture—are related to these structures by which God preserves the world is something that Christians need to look at more seriously.

Canadian artist Michael Snow has said about his art: I make the rules of the game by which I play. If I begin losing, I change the rules. As moderns, we are inclined to see life this way. We create the game and change the rules when it suits us. The Christian vision is different. Some understand this vision to be like a jigsaw puzzle in which the outcome is predetermined (little freedom here).

Owen Meany, in John Irving's *A Prayer for Owen Meany*, has a strong sense of God's providence in jigsaw puzzle terms. I find myself almost persuaded by Owen Meany. There is an intractability about our world and our individual personalities. In the end, however, I find the Scrabble game metaphor to be more faithful to the Judeo-Christian vision (see chapter 1). It allows for a maximum amount of dynamic freedom for human beings within a structure, a set of limitations, by which we ourselves are measured.

No, God does not play dice with the world.

10

SALVATION PART ONE
Yasch Siemens
or George Brunk?

I N 1984, NOVELIST ARMIN WIEBE CAUSED A STIR IN southern Manitoba with his Mennonite classic, *The Salvation of Yasch Siemens.* People seemed to find Wiebe's depiction of Mennonite village life—with its mixture of fantasy and realism, sex and religion, Low German and English, beer and church testimonies—just too threatening.

Having grown up in southern Manitoba myself, I found Wiebe to have captured the ethos of Mennonite life on the prairies more accurately than anything I had yet read. What most fascinated me was Wiebe's portrayal of the meaning of salvation for Yasch (Jake) Siemens. No dramatic conversions for this sinner. No "going to the front" at a Brunk campaign. No struggle with guilt and sin. No sudden deliverance.

Salvation for Yasch begins with Oata Needarp, a woman who weighs over 200 pounds but is to inherit a half section of land. His fantasies over skinny Sadie Nickel gradually recede as Oata takes over, indulges him with chokecherry wine, and takes him to Christian Endeavour meetings in church.

Yasch's tragic-comic testimony in front of the church, a precondition for marriage, falls far short of any ideal. The couple marries, has children, farms, goes to church, and lives an average existence. Salvation for the *dow-nix* (good-for-nothing) Yasch Siemens comes with growing up, experiencing love and affection, discovering his modest place in life, and becoming a responsible member of his community. In the end, his eyes are opened to the realization that life is not so bad after all.

During the 1950s, when I was growing up in this same community, an American Mennonite revivalist named George R. Brunk II took the community by storm with a completely different message of salvation. It was a message that was to shape the religious sensibility of a whole generation of young people (including my own), both for good and for bad.

Brunk was a larger-than-life figure whose caravan of trucks, massive tent, and powerful rhetoric brought change to traditional Mennonite communal culture, language, and theology. Salvation in the Brunk model was to recognize one's sin, guilt, and lost state. One had to be converted—a dramatic about-face in one's life that came with surrender to God and putting one's faith in Christ.

Salvation was something unusual, extraordinary, an interruption in the humdrum existence of the Yasch Siemens variety. There can be no doubt that this message of salvation—with authentic biblical and historical antecedents in Paul, Augustine, Luther, Wesley, and Chuck Colson—was a liberation for many.

For some of us, however, it exacted a great price: years of self-doubt, neurosis, even despair. In my case, one half of my religious temperament came from the Sommerfelder-Bergthaler West Reserve Yasch Siemens variety. The other half was inherited from the Kleinegemeinde-Steinbach East Reserve kind of Mennonite sensibility, the Brunk variety. This second half predisposed me to a highly introspective, guilt-ridden spirituality and made me especially vulnerable to the salvation message of evangelists such as Barry Moore, Jack Wurtzen, and George Brunk.

I went to the front many times, prayed and confessed without ceasing, experienced numerous "conversions," always in the vain search for religious ecstasy and certainty. Salvation for me came in unexpected ways. It took years of intense study and growth in self-understanding, aided by psychotherapy. With marriage, having a family, and experiencing a sense of belonging in a professional and religious community came greater understanding. My eyes were gradually opened to the meaning of salvation.

I am indebted to the Brunk message of salvation—my passion for theology derives from it. I lament the fact that my children know little of that era and its truths. My generation has been so determined not to subject our children to hell-fire salvation, that we have domesticated Christianity far too much.

The Bible has many images for salvation: liberation (Luke 4:18); living right (Luke 18:18–23), forgiveness (Acts 2:38), healing (1 Peter 2:24), and new birth (John 3:3). The image that best describes my own experience, however, is that of a blind man receiving his sight (John 9), having my eyes gradually opened to see how Christ is present in our lives and in the world (Luke 24:31).

In the next chapter, I will look at a theological understanding of salvation as the restoration of humanity and the world to that which God intended at creation.

11

SALVATION PART TWO
Did Jesus Die for My Sins?

S | ALVATION—YASCH SIEMENS VARIETY OR GEORGE
Brunk variety? That is how I framed the alternatives
in the last chapter.

Yasch Siemens is not inclined to talk easily about salvation, let alone the assurance of salvation. One gradually finds one's place within the community and does the best one can. God takes care of the rest. For George Brunk, salvation is a conscious choice, including recognition of one's sinfulness, repentance, turning in faith to Jesus Christ for the forgiveness of one's sins, and conversion to a new way of life. Here salvation is a dramatic interruption in ordinary life, a new way of being, and certainty is attainable.

A critic once pointed out that I offer these two as equally legitimate ways of salvation. True, I do not say one is right and the other wrong. Nor do I identify exclusively with one or the other. My religious sensibility has been shaped by both.

The biblical metaphor that best reflects my view of salvation, however, is the blind man gradually receiving sight (John 9). Other biblical metaphors—liberation, forgiveness, healing—all concentrate on the human subject. The "receiving of sight" image, however, is the coming into view of something beyond ourselves. We are not on our own. This image points to the belief that something is going on in the cosmos beyond ourselves, but of which we are a part. Salvation is illumination, our eyes being opened to what God is already doing in the world and in our lives.

What is it that God is doing? Restoring fallen creation: the visible and the invisible, the heavens, the earth and vegetation, moon and stars, birds and fish, animals and human beings.

Unity best describes the unfallen (prelapsarian) world of Genesis 1. Not everything is the same, or equal, but there is harmony and interconnectedness among all levels of creation. Separation (or estrangement) best reflects the fall so dramatically narrated in Genesis 3. This fall (a way of saying that all human beings sin) has universal consequences: alienation between humans and God (Adam and Eve hide from God), between humans and humans (Adam dominates Eve), between humans and animals (Eve accuses the serpent), between humans and non-human nature (thorns and thistles frustrate human labor), between nature and nature (the ground is cursed).

The whole family of terms having to do with salvation (redemption, regeneration, justification, sanctification) has to do with the restoration of the world to the original vision in which all parts are integrated to make a unified whole, with God as "ground" (source) of being.

Eating from the tree of the knowledge of good and evil represents human beings wanting to know too much, to have absolute knowledge of the mysteries, the part wanting to be the whole (the definition of heresy). Eating of the tree of life represents restoration. God drives Adam and Eve out of the garden lest they eat of this tree. Restoration is not at human disposal; it is by divine initiative.

Jesus Christ represents this tree of life for the Christian community. One of the most common ways of speaking about God's restoration of creation is that Jesus died on the cross for the sins of the world. Does this language have any meaning for us today? Does it still have symbolic power?

The substitutionary-satisfaction theory of atonement has biblical roots (Galatians 3:10-14), but was systematically formulated by Anselm in the eleventh century. Behind it lies the notion that we deserve punishment and death for our sins against a righteous God. God sent his son to die on our behalf, according to this theory, thus appeasing God's wrath. This model corresponds to a legal view of sin as disobedience to God's laws; this disobedience needs to be dealt with in God's judicial court.

This is but one way of talking about how God restores the world. Another is the relational model (John 3:16, 2 Corinthians 5:14–19), sometimes referred to as the moral influence theory, articulated by Abelard in the twelfth century. In this view, Christ's death on the cross represents not appeasement of divine wrath, but the reconciling love of God for the world. This corresponds to a view of sin as the breaking of relationship(s).

A third is the older Christus Victor model in which Christ's death and resurrection represent the victory of the cosmic force of good over evil (Colossians 2:15, 20, Hebrews 2:14–15). A modern version of this theory interprets Christ's death and resurrection in historical, political terms—Christ liberates people from the structures of political oppression and domination.

All three models have biblical support, but the legal substitutionary-satisfaction model probably gives us the most difficulty today. Can we still talk about Jesus dying for our sins without making God into a vengeful murderer or a "divine child abuser," as some feminists have put it?

Yes we can! But not if we think of Jesus as a kind of second, lesser god whom God sacrifices. This is polytheism. The substitutionary model can be meaningful only if we understand Christ's death on the cross as God himself dying on our behalf, bearing our sins.

This is the resurrection of the world through divine suffering. But this is only one side of God. The importance of a trinitarian view of God is that God has a number of sides, including a judging and a loving side. The strength of the substitutionary-satisfaction language is that it takes sin and evil seriously. Behind this way of speaking is the conviction that we cannot save ourselves and need forgiveness.

Elie Wiesel recounts how in Auschwitz, Jewish inmates were forced to watch the hanging of three fellow prisoners. One, a young boy, suffered longer than the two older men because he was so light. Elie heard one observer cry out: "Where is Yahweh now?"

"There, hanging on the scaffold," came the reply from another prisoner. In Christ, God suffers for and with the world, thereby restoring it. How this restoration happens in our broken world will be the topic of a future chapter.

12

SANCTIFICATION
Do People Get Better as They Get Older?

I N ONE OF HIS SONGS, CANADIAN MINISTREL LEONARD Cohen laments the lack of human perfection: "The birds they sang at the break of day / Start again I heard them say / Don't dwell on what has passed away or what is yet to be." The recurring refrain: "Ring the bells that still can ring / Forget your perfect offering / There is a crack in everything / That's how the light gets in."

The realization that as one gets older one does not necessarily become wiser, more generous or spiritual (more loving toward God and others) can be quite disillusioning. One's illusions about great achievements, professional excellence, and spiritual perfection are shattered as physical and mental strength deteriorate.

Some people develop a dignity and graciousness of spirit as they age (I have met them), but many, even those who have practiced spiritual disciplines of prayer and Bible reading throughout life, struggle more intensely with the "deadly sins" than ever before. (The seven deadly sins are pride, covetousness, lust, envy, gluttony, anger, and sloth.)

So what about the theological doctrine of "sanctification"? The word means growth in personal holiness, made possible through the work of the Holy Spirit in one's life. "Regeneration" is the transformation of character through the Spirit that makes sanctification possible. Sanctification is the process of becoming Christ-like in daily life—manifesting the fruits of the spirit and appropriating the virtues. (The "cardinal virtues" are justice, prudence, temperance and fortitude, rounded out by the theological virtues of faith, hope, and charity.)

There's been a lot of talk in Anabaptist circles in recent years about "character formation." Courses in spirituality and the practice of spiritual direction (where a spiritual mentor acts as a guide and confessor) have become common. These have helped us retrieve some of the riches of the Catholic heritage. Catholics and Anabaptists share an interest in spiritual formation. Each emphasizes the importance of both justifying grace (being made righteous in the eyes of God) and sanctifying grace in the process of salvation, within the context of the church.

In contrast, some of the sixteenth-century reformers, especially Luther, were so intent on emphasizing justification by grace through faith alone, that sanctification received hardly any attention. There was considerable debate between the Anabaptists and the Lutherans on this subject.

It is interesting that eighteenth-century Pietists retrieved a strong emphasis on sanctification and upright living within Lutheranism. In the Holiness and Pentecostal traditions, double and even triple works of grace (justification, sanctification, and speaking in tongues) became important tests of faith.

Mennonites in their call to discipleship have a lot in common with traditions that are serious about sanctification (holy living). Anabaptist literature speaks repeatedly about regeneration by the Holy Spirit and taking on the nature of Christ in daily life. This had important implications for the Mennonite view of the church as pure, "without spot and blemish." This doctrine of the church tended toward a perfectionism that often had devastating results, the topic of the next chapter. In real life, the church falls far short of this ideal.

I'm all for sanctification, but my problem is I'm not sure I would recognize holiness were I to see it. There are no easy criteria to determine who is sanctified and who is not. I do know that the people I find most inspiring are not the "nicest" or most "spiritual," but are often unlikely characters who become means of divine grace for others in spite of themselves.

As a Mennonite, I find it extremely liberating to read Luther and experience something of that "live boldly" approach for which he is so famous. Not "sin boldly that grace may abound" but "live boldly that grace may abound" might be our motto. To live boldly gets one enmeshed in the ambiguities (and sins) for which one needs forgiveness and the grace of God.

As we get older we frequently lose our inhibitions, shed our pretensions, and say what's on our minds—not usually what we think of as sanctified living. The doctrine of sanctification is a noble teaching, spurring us on to strive after virtue. It's when holiness becomes too rigidly defined, a burden that weighs us down, or a saccharine sanctimony, that we have lost it.

Is it not precisely as imperfect human beings that God loves us? Our sanctity is not a painstaking human achievement. It is a series of momentary intimations of divine grace within daily, mundane existence.

"There is a crack in everything. That's how the light gets in."

13

THE CHURCH PART ONE
With Spot and Wrinkle

I N *THE SHUNNING,* MENNONITE POET PATRICK Friesen tells the story of the church's excommunication and shunning (avoidance) of Peter, an independent, stubborn farmer. Peter's sin is his pride and his refusal to bow to the will of the church's leaders. In the end, Peter is totally isolated from his community. Even his wife who loves him dearly is under strict orders not to associate with him. He commits suicide.

To his credit, Friesen paints an empathetic picture not only of Peter and his family, but also of the church. He powerfully portrays what can happen in a tightly controlled religious community where the so-called common good is put before the freedom of the individual. The danger increases when the guardians of this community hold up as their motto the perfectionism of Ephesians 5:27: "so as to present the church to himself in splendor, without spot or wrinkle or anything of the kind—yes, so that she may be holy and without blemish."

My grandfather, another Peter, suffered under the harsh treatment of such a community, without opportunity for self-defense. After ten years in the ministry, he was defrocked and excommunicated for doctrinal reasons, but personality conflicts were clearly involved. In the mid-1970s I taped his account of his growing up years in southern Manitoba, his innovative approach to youth work, his years of ministry, and his later difficulties with the church leadership.

Attempts at reconciliation were unsuccessful. Although I could not agree with some of his theological views, my respect for this gentle man increased as I listened to his sad story. I realized how difficult it was for the Mennonite church in previous generations to tolerate diversity of opinion and belief.

This is especially ironic seeing that our Anabaptist ancestors were among the first to emphasize the freedom of religion within society. They expected tolerance from the outside but could not tolerate diversity within their own membership. Had Anabaptism existed at the time of the great debate between the Augustinians and the Donatists (fourth and fifth centuries), it without a doubt would have sided with the "heretical" Donatists. The Donatists were the most rigorous in their belief in the pure, uncompromising church, unwilling to readmit the backsliders who had lapsed during persecution.

As a consequence of this rigid view of the church, Mennonites have seen more splits than most other groups. The price we have paid for our strong emphasis on holy living (sanctification) is division, for, as a Dutch Mennonite theologian has noted, emphasizing sanctification divides while an emphasis on justification (grace) unites.

This is our heritage as Mennonites—the legacy of a persecuted minority group whose identity could only be maintained through strict discipline and perfectionist ideals. It no longer describes our present reality. We have lost our innocence in this regard. We have come to realize that the world is within us. Does this mean that we ought to give up our historical vision of discipleship?

In 1994, I sat in the pews of one of the oldest Mennonite churches in the world, the United Mennonite (Doops-gezinde) Congregation of Haarlem, The Netherlands, built in 1683. It is in this region that the Anabaptist-Mennonite vision of the visible church without wrinkle or blemish took shape.

For Menno Simons, this view was based on the questionable doctrine that the incarnation occurred without Christ partaking of Mary's flesh. Jesus was born through Mary, but without being blemished by her humanity. He called this Christ's "celestial flesh." And, since the church was viewed as the body of Christ, it also was to be without spot, wrinkle, or blemish. By the seventeenth century, Dutch Mennonites, many of them wealthy and integrated into society, had given up this pure church ideal. Their assimilation is graphically documented in a 1994 Dutch publication provocatively entitled *From Martyr to Muppy*.

Most Mennonite churches in North America have in recent decades followed the Dutch example. They have opted for a liberal view of the church in which individual freedom of belief and behavior takes priority over a communal ethic. Or is the very notion of individual freedom an illusion? Have we simply adopted new forms of social control determined by our age? We may have exorcized one set of demons from our tradition—excommunication and shunning—only to replace it with another set.

As Mennonites in this new millennium, we need to reexamine our doctrine of the church. Is it not possible to develop a theology of the church (ecclesiology) that holds in creative tension individual freedom and communal solidarity, diversity and high ethical standards, justification (recognition of our fallenness) and sanctification (pursuit of holiness)?

14

THE CHURCH PART TWO

Mennonites and Other Catholics

O NE OF THE MOST PRESSING QUESTIONS FOR YOUNG people thinking about joining the church, I have found, is how they can be sure that ours is the "right" religion. Youth are more critical than adults of the infighting, factionalism, and intolerance among religious groups, and open to searching for truth wherever it may be found.

The Apostles' Creed is the most universally accepted of all Christian confessions. Anabaptists, like other Christian groups at the time of Reformation, used its three main articles (God, Christ, Holy Spirit) subdivided into twelve affirmations of faith.

One of these affirmations states: "I believe in the Holy Spirit, the holy catholic Church, the communion of saints. . . ." What does it mean to believe in the "holy catholic church"? Catholic has come to be identified with Roman Catholics, but really it means "universal." Mennonites are part of this universal (catholic) church. This is an important realization for a church that frequently thinks of itself as separate from, even "over against," other parts of the Christian tradition.

The concept of the church has its roots in the Old Testament notion of the covenant. The tower of Babel story (Genesis 11) begins with all people having one language, and ends with the world fragmented into many different groups and languages because of human arrogance. The story of the Hebrew people is the story of God's covenant with a particular group which is to be the means of God's blessing (salvation, reconciliation) to the "multitude of nations" (Genesis 17). It is a colorful story of regression into pagan idolatries and narrow nationalism.

There are also accounts, like the book of Ruth, of rising above tribalism, and showing kindness to the stranger. A minority of Jews, particularly the prophets, keep alive a more universal vision of a messianic age of peace, justice, and reconciliation.

A small group of first-century Jewish-Christians confessed that Jesus was the Christ (Messiah)—the one to usher in the universal kingdom of God, in which there is neither Jew nor Greek, slave nor free, male nor female (Galatians 3:28). The main conflict within this Jewish-Christian community, and between this community and the other Jews, had to do with the universal nature of the Jewish heritage in Christ (see Acts 10 and 15).

The birth of the New Testament church at Pentecost (Acts 2) is the reversal of Babel. Here people from every nation, each speaking in their own language, could understand each other. Here was miraculous reconciliation and mutual understanding without giving up difference. This is the characteristic work of the Spirit. Throughout the Old and New Testaments the basic character of the divine Spirit is to work through the many different groups to create unity without destroying diversity. The idea of the church as one body with many different parts, each with its distinctive function but united through the Holy Spirit, is an important metaphor for Paul (1 Corinthians 12).

The tension between the call to unity and the respect for diversity has been the thorn in the flesh of the church throughout history. Always there has been the temptation to stifle dissenting voices and enforce an oppressive unity or to break apart into irreconcilable factions.

The first disciples of Jesus were not immune to internal squabbling, petty jealousies, denial, betrayal, and power struggles. The first major conference in Jerusalem (Acts 15) depicts the early Christians divided between the legalists and non-legalists, exclusivists and inclusivists. After heated discussion and the Spirit's leading, they were able to come to some agreement.

In the Middle Ages it was the Orthodox against the Roman Catholics, with a few small dissenting sects. After the Reformation it was the Catholics, Anglicans, Reformed, Lutherans, and Anabaptists all against each other. By now, untold groups each claim to have the truth. Mennonites themselves are divided into some twenty-five or more different groups in Canada alone.

The church as filled by the Spirit can legitimately be said to be the continuation of the being (body) and work of Christ in the world. In Ephesians 4, Paul describes the church as the "household of God" in which those who were far off, divided, alienated, strangers to the covenants of promise, are given equal access in one Spirit to God.

We Mennonites need seriously to consider what this means for our relationship with other Mennonites, other Christians, and other religions. How can we be open to the witness of other groups while remaining faithful to the affirmations of our own tradition? Eastern Orthodox Christians have something to teach us about the mystical-spiritual view of reality, Catholics about unity and the sacraments, Anglicans about liturgy and worship, Lutherans about grace, the Reformed about the sovereignty of God over all of creation, and Pentecostals about the Spirit.

Our historic emphasis on discipleship, peace, and community is a witness that we need to share rigorously with others while recognizing that it is not the whole gospel.

15

SACRAMENTS
Does God Come to Us Through the Material World?

BAPTISM AND COMMUNION WERE SACRAMENTAL occasions for me when I first experienced them in the Bergthaler Mennonite Church, even though I had never heard the term "sacrament." They continue to be times when God's grace comes to me through physical objects, people, and events.

I remember those next to me ritualistically nodding at each other before sipping their sweet *Manischewitz* (interestingly, a kosher wine) and reverently enfolding the bread in their clean, white handkerchiefs before corporately partaking of what they considered in some sense to be the very body of Christ. The mystery was lessened by the knowledge that my father, as deacon of the church, was in charge of purchasing and storing the wine in our basement, and mother, together with other deacons' wives, spent a good part of Saturday baking communion bread.

Yet, the wine and bread took on a symbolic power once they were consecrated by the minister. Only later did I learn that Mennonites, unlike some other faith groups, did not really believe that these elements were Christ's body and blood but were signs by which to remember what Christ had done for us, and a challenge for us to follow his example. And yet, I always felt that maybe the sacramentalists were right.

Fierce controversies have raged over the sacraments. Heretics have been burned at the stake for denying the "Real Presence" in the bread and wine. Churches have been divided over how many sacraments there ought to be (two, three, or seven), how they ought to be administered, and whether their effectiveness depends on the integrity of the person administering them.

Some Christian groups (Quakers, Salvation Army) have rejected their use altogether. Mennonites have preferred to use the term "ordinances" (practices directly instituted by Jesus).

The word "sacrament" came into Christian usage around the third century, combining the Latin *sager* (holy) with the Greek *mysterion* (mystery). It came to mean that holy mystery and power transmitted through material means and rituals. "Take, eat; this is my body. . . . Drink of it, all of you; for this is my blood of the covenant." With these words, Jesus at the Last Supper instituted the basic rite of the Christian church, called the agape meal, Lord's Supper, or eucharist.

The medieval church accepted seven sacramental rites: baptism, confirmation, eucharist, penance, holy orders, matrimony, and extreme unction. Even some Mennonite groups, for whom baptism and the Lord's Supper were the central rites, in time identified seven ordinances taught by the New Testament: baptism, Lord's Supper, foot washing, holy kiss, anointing with oil, prayer veiling, and marriage (with the possibility of an eighth: laying on of hands at ordination).

Battle lines between Catholics, Lutherans, Calvinists, and Anabaptists were drawn during the Reformation over the meaning of these sacraments. Was "this is my body" to be taken literally (transubstantiation), paradoxically (consubstantiation), figuratively (spiritually), or memorially ("Do this in remembrance of me")? The last tended to be the Anabaptist-Mennonite view, but there was much more at stake than simply how to interpret the elements of communion. Mennonites had trouble with the whole sacerdotal (priestly) tradition in which special individuals with sacred status and powers were the official dispensers of divine grace.

Is any of this important for us today? Yes it is. What is at stake is how we view the material world—the world of the senses—in relation to the divine. Things have reversed themselves from the time of the Reformation, when the world was experienced as spirit-filled (enchanted). There were in the late Middle Ages a host of sacred places, sacred objects, sacred times, and sacred persons.

With the rise of the modern world, nature, at least in western culture, has become disenchanted or de-spirited. We manipulate nature as though it were "dead stuff" to be used for our purposes. Nature sometimes revolts against our attempts to control it. For example, new organisms introduced into alien environments can drastically upset the ecosystem and threaten our world. Potentially, nature can be the medium of divine grace, but for Christians it can never itself be considered divine.

Fortunately, there are signs of renewal in our attitude towards nature. It is a good time for Mennonites to re-examine the way we understand our "ordinances." How we view these central rites of the worshiping community has something to do with how we understand the material world around us, and whether we believe the divine comes to us through the physical senses, not just through word and text.

16

BAPTISM

An Antiquated Initiation Rite?

MY FIRST RECOLLECTION OF A SERIOUS ARGUMENT over baptism was in a raspberry patch in Yarrow, British Columbia. I was fifteen years old and on a vacation from Manitoba, picking fruit with my family to help pay our way. The owner of the fruit farm was a Mennonite Brethren minister, passionately committed to baptism by immersion. Dad, a "sprinkler," was not about to admit that the mode of baptism was all that important. In those days there still seemed to be something at stake in such theological debate.

Until recently, it was taken for granted that when young people reached a certain age they would consider baptism. It was a kind of initiation rite, not only into the institutional church, but into the Mennonite community. Often baptism was considered a requisite for getting married. This assumed a tightly-knit ethnic Mennonite community with the church at the center. Adult baptism was a rite of passage, and marriage and family life were nurtured in a community defined by church.

For the most part, we no longer live with these assumptions. No longer is the Mennonite community ethnically homogeneous. No longer can one assume that marriage is a church-related "sacrament." Intermarriage between "infant baptizers" and "adult baptizers" has blurred the lines even further.

The institutional church has lost its significance for a large number of young urban professionals who were raised with the old assumptions. One of these recently approached me with the strange query: Is it possible to be unbaptized?

Today many successful Mennonite professionals live on the margins of the church. Their children are rarely encouraged to go to church, let alone confronted with the need to make a religious choice and be baptized. The institutional church has become largely irrelevant for these people. They feel nothing is going on.

For many people, there is something anachronistic about theological debates over sixteenth-century convictions about adult baptism versus infant baptism. For them, Balthasar Hubmaier's three types of baptism—by spirit, water, and fire (martyrdom)—have little significance. (They would find even more absurd the proposal of one of my graduate professors that perhaps "computers should be baptized.")

Even within the institutional church there is frequently confusion over, and even outright resistance to, confronting young people with the importance of making religious choices and considering baptism. There is a great fear of putting pressure on people and defining church membership too rigidly, thinking better to err on the side of openness, tolerance, informality, and a blurring of the lines.

In my own zeal to draw young people into catechetical instruction in my congregation and to give them the option of being baptized, I was reproached by one senior member who told me this was un-Anabaptist. An Anabaptist does not try to persuade people to make such choices, he said, but leaves that up to the Spirit.

When our Anabaptist free-choice/adult baptism approach gets aligned with a modern culture that avoids anything that smacks of religious pressure, what is the result? We are left with the road of least resistance in which young people are seldom even given the occasion to consider becoming Christians and recognizing this through baptism.

Should we give up baptism altogether? Is it an antiquated initiation rite, based on an outmoded theology, for a community that no longer exists? No. This may be the most propitious moment within the Mennonite community to rethink in imaginative ways the mystery of baptism. It is one of those few "sacramental" occasions in the life of the Mennonite church when young people are confronted with the seriousness of faith, the need to become responsible adults and to make some religious decisions.

I find young people remarkably open to the great religious questions and to the rituals of the church. But there has to be a sense that something is going on here, a sense that the church is not afraid to address the difficult challenges of modern culture and of other traditions. A sense that here one finds genuine people facing moral challenges, finding forgiveness, and experiencing spiritual power.

Baptism then is not a nail in the coffin, or a melodramatic crossing of the finish line, but a mark along the way. It is a deliberate choice to travel with others the human journey of faith.

17

PRAYER

God Speaking Through Us to God

WHEN IT COMES TO PRAYER, PLATITUDES ABOUND! WE slip into easy formulas, one of which is the "Jesus wejus" style (as in "Jesus we jus(t) ask you to. . . ."), a kind of groveling plea for one more thing from a busy deity.

Worship, prayer, devotion, and other acts of piety are indispensable in religious life, and are the basis of love and discipleship (the topic of the next chapter). But what is one to say about them? So much that passes for prayer is little more than vanity, rhetoric, self-indulgence, superstition, or manipulation of God.

Many of us grew up in families where Bible reading and devotions were daily rituals, and where a private devotional life was encouraged. As a child I read the Bible diligently, memorizing large sections (usually for camp), prayed at length, sometimes under my blankets with hands over eyes and ears to shut out the world, occasionally falling asleep on my knees. My prayer lists were long—for missionaries, family, cousins, and especially for those still "unsaved."

Virtually every type of prayer can be found in the Bible: prayer for vindication and deliverance (Psalm 43), prayer as unrelenting struggle with God (Genesis 32:28), prayer as defiance and desperation (Job 7), prayer for the enemy (Matthew 5.44), prayer for one's abusers (Luke 6:28), prayer for those in need (1 Corinthians 1:9), prayer for miraculous healing (Acts 9:40), prayers for military victory, material necessities, confession, and thanksgiving. The prototype of all prayers is, of course, the Lord's Prayer (Matthew 6:9–13).

Apostle Paul makes an interesting point when he says, "I will pray with the spirit, but I will pray with the mind also" (1 Corinthians 14:15). We bring to prayer not only our emotions, but our intellects. Furthermore, prayer in the deepest sense is a search for the wisdom and knowledge of God.

Behind all the ancient prayers is the conviction that there is a personal, divine reality who has power, is in control of things, and whose will we are to discern and follow. We are accountable to a higher reality. Furthermore, prayer makes a difference to what God is doing in the world.

Childlike prayers of petition (asking for things) are biblical and important, but they can easily become self-indulgent. Prayer is often reduced to a type of group therapy. We pray to ourselves or to each other, believing that prayer is effective not only in "moving the arms of God," but in doing something positive to us. Then there are those who occasionally revert to superstitious-like prayer. For example, my cynical friend who prays when he flies to a conference, "Please don't let this plane crash."

So how do we pray? The issue is really how do we understand God? One temptation is to think of God in totally objective, distant terms—a father figure in the sky to whom we kowtow and whom we consult on every little thing, thereby losing our sense of dignity and responsibility. Or we think of God in totally subjective terms—the divine spark within us, so that praying is little more than talking to ourselves, a projection of our own desires.

In our time, when most everything is defined in terms of technique (efficiency as the highest value), prayer tends to become a technical act. How is it possible to pray in such an age as ours, that is, to open ourselves up to the Other in a non-technical way? To be listeners and recipients rather than actors?

There is frequent confusion about whether one is praying to God, to Jesus, or to the Holy Spirit. Prayer is communion with God in God's threefoldness:

1. In praying we contemplate the divine mystery, that which is beyond ourselves.

2. We meditate on this mystery as made known to us in the Christ-event.

3. We open ourselves up to the present power of this divine reality as God's Spirit meets our spirit.

This mystery transcends us, yet is closer to us than we are to ourselves. It is our very ground and center. Prayer is to find our own ground in God and to open ourselves to what God is already doing in the world.

Theologian Paul Tillich has suggested that prayer is "God (as Spirit) speaking through us to God." In prayer not only are we communing with God, God is communing with God. Perhaps this is what Paul means when he says, "Likewise the Spirit helps us in our weakness; for we do not know how to pray as we ought, but that very Spirit intercedes for us with sighs too deep for words" (Romans 8:26).

Karl Marx once said, "The philosophers have thought about the world long enough; now it is time to change it." He got his wish. The last two centuries have seen a fanatical obsession with human action—much of it in the name of improving the world (progress) at the price of thought. And look where it has got us.

Maybe it's time to reverse Marx's aphorism: "We have acted upon (dominated) the world long enough; now it's time to meditate upon it." Prayer, above all, is the loving contemplation of God and what God is doing in the world.

18

LOVE
Who Is the Enemy?

WHILE LIVING IN BAVARIA IN 1995, MY FAMILY AND I walked forty-five minutes to attend a Catholic service in a restored Benedictine monastery founded in 1119. All around us were plaques, tombs of bishops, princes and saints, and striking wall paintings dating back to the twelfth century. A portrait of Emperor Charles V (the persecutor of Anabaptists) adorned the chancel.

What was the theme of the morning? Loving the enemy! Makes one wonder.

We were living in Regensburg, one of the hot spots of sixteenth-century Anabaptist activity. Balthasar Hubmaier, an important Anabaptist theologian, was the main preacher in the local Cathedral of St. Peter before his conversion. He was known for his strong anti-Semitism and was responsible for destroying the local synagogue in 1519 and raising a chapel in honor of the Virgin Mary on the same spot. Shortly after, this chapel was replaced by a Lutheran church in which I preached on Palm Sunday. What should one say?

The Benedictine priest we had heard earlier dwelt on two issues. What kind of love is meant when talking about loving the enemy? And how can the enemy still remain an enemy after we love him or her? Love for the enemy is a divine love, quite different from erotic love (man and woman) and familial love (parent and child), he said. It is the kind of love than can transform an enemy into a friend.

The sermon was good, but it remained totally on the level of personal relationships. It made me realize how rich is our Anabaptist-Mennonite heritage of discipleship. We have tried to apply nonviolent love to social, political, and economic realms, not just to individual morality.

As a Mennonite I have been indoctrinated by one central conviction: We do not go to war, no matter what. Why? Because this is what Jesus taught. This is an essential part of discipleship *(Nachfolge)*. With time I learned how to make distinctions between "liberal" pacifism and "biblical" nonresistance (Mennonites held to the latter). I learned to use the jargon and talk knowledgeably about self-sacrificial love, agape, nonviolent resistance, peacemaking, shalom, and reconciliation.

Meanwhile I began teaching a course on "War and peace in Christian theology," with students from many traditions in my classes. It confirmed my growing awareness that not all Christians share my views, and that the Bible can be interpreted in different ways. One can find texts to support Holy War, Just War, and almost any position. I have also realized that Christians other than Mennonites have a commitment to nonviolence and to peacemaking.

Nor are Mennonites themselves of one mind. Early Anabaptists disagreed on the use of violence: some supported outright use of arms to bring in the kingdom (Münsterites), some advocated postponing violence until the end

(Hans Hut), some accepted conditional violence to defend the state (Hubmaier), and even those who believed Christians should be nonviolent (Conrad Grebel and Menno Simons) did not deny the state's right to use violence to protect the good and punish evil.

Perhaps most disturbing is the realization that none of us is consistent. We may have defended the nonviolent love ethic in public but lived by another standard in private— for example, abusive relationships in the home. Psychologists and counselors have brought us a new understanding of the depths of the anger and violence within ourselves, and their neurotic manifestations. Our writers, such as Rudy Wiebe, have shown how peace has destroyed many. Feminists have argued that our emphasis on self-sacrificial love has been exploitative when applied to those already oppressed.

I am reminded of the powerful scene in Al Reimer's *My Harp Is Turned to Mourning* where the Mennonite minister comes face to face with the enemy, Nestor Machno. What is most striking about the dialogue between these two is that the terrorist Machno is revealed to be the minister's alter ego, the dark side of the Mennonite psyche.

Who is the enemy? The Catholic? The Fundamentalist? The Muslim? The Parent? The Employer? The Institution? It is interesting that Jesus takes for granted that we have enemies. But Jesus also tells us to look first at ourselves (Matthew 7:1–5). It is the enemy within ourselves and within our own community that we are called to face. Only as we experience the transforming love and forgiveness of God ourselves are we freed to love the other. Frequently the other becomes the mirror in which we come to see ourselves as we really are.

At the heart of the gospel is the difficult love ethic of Jesus. We dare not domesticate (soften) the Jesus who followed the way of the cross and called us to do the same. Let us pass on to our children our rich Anabaptist-Mennonite heritage, and bring our insights to the ecumenical table.

But let us not be self-righteous and hypocritical. We do not have a monopoly on the gospel, nor is nonviolence a trump card that we can pull out whenever useful in an argument with other Christians. We have too many skeletons in our closets to claim any superiority.

19

SEXUALITY
The Erotic and the Divine

W HY ARE WE SO CAPTIVATED BY ALL THINGS SEXUAL? IS Freud right after all—that life is ultimately to be understood in terms of our sexual drives and that to repress these is the cause of all our neuroses?

Familiar to every one of us are the biblical prescriptions against the sins of the flesh—lust, licentiousness, fornication, adultery, sodomy, and various forms of sexual perversion— all those words that titillated our imaginations in Sunday school. Our Mennonite confessions of faith usually have a separate article on marriage and family, emphasizing the legitimate place of sexuality within monogamous, heterosexual "covenants."

And yet we keep on testing the boundaries of human sexuality in our relations with others. We are curious, take risks, flirt with life, and explore new possibilities (as though tempting the gods). Why is this? Perhaps because the excitement of sexuality is in its danger, its explosive power, its refusal to be domesticated. Sex brings us to the very origin of life (and also death). Herein lies its attraction and its tragedy.

This is why, in some religions, sexuality has been placed at the center of worship (e.g. fertility cults) as the means through which one encounters the divine. Sexual ecstasy has often been thought to be an experience of transcendence.

In contemporary Christian theology, talk about "God as mother," the world as "God's body," and creation as "God giving birth" tend in this direction. Greater value is given to the body, the sensual, and the erotic—a legitimate reaction to the cold, rational, distant male God that has frequently dominated our theology and our worship.

Nevertheless, in an age prone to fixation on the human body we need to ask ourselves: where does the erotic fit into the scheme of things? Is sexual union between a man and a woman an intimation of union with the divine? Is sexual ecstasy a religious experience? As Mennonites we have tended, in good Protestant fashion, to separate totally sexual experience and the encounter with the divine. We have defined divine love as agape—the unconditional love of the other for his or her own sake. This ideal form of love is portrayed as the model for all human relations.

Our view of discipleship (including self-sacrificial love) is premised on this model of pure, divine love. As a result, we are at a loss where to place erotic love (eros: the desire for the other as a way to complete ourselves).

Interestingly, the Catholic tradition (which has so strongly emphasized celibacy as the ideal) has embraced the centrality of the senses more openly than Protestants have. Smell, touch, and taste have a significant place in Catholic worship, and church art depicts the sensuous, even erotic, human body in the context of the great religious themes. Marriage (including sexuality) is given sacramental status (a means of divine grace) in the Catholic church.

What makes the Bible (particularly the Hebrew Scriptures) such compelling literature is that it deals with the full range of human experience, including startling sexual encounters: the nakedness of Noah (Genesis 9), Abraham and Hagar (Genesis 16), Lot and his daughters (Genesis 19), David's many concubines (2 Samuel 16), and his affair with Bathsheba (2 Samuel 11).

Both Jews and Christians have been embarrassed by the explicitly erotic language of the Song of Solomon and have offered spiritualized interpretations of these love songs (e.g. they are really about the church's relation to God or the soul's dialogue with the divine). Yet, there they remain as part of our sacred text, testifying to the validity of the erotic for Judeo-Christian anthropology.

Even the New Testament (which is much narrower in its portrayal of human experience than is the Old Testament) uses marriage imagery as a metaphor for human-divine relationships (2 Corinthians 11, Ephesians 5, Revelation 21).

We tend to tear asunder divine love and human love. Erotic love can have spiritual meaning for us, however, if its physical-sexual expression is not absolutized, if it does not take on first importance. This is why the tradition of celibacy, chastity, and singleness (illustrated by Jesus and Paul) is significant. It reminds us of the relative (derivative) importance of sexual expression.

Erotic love is the desire for the other as complement to and fulfillment of the self. This is to be distinguished from physical lust (the use of another for self-gratification). One sees the difference when one compares authentic art and sexual exploitation on television. In good art, the erotic always points beyond the purely physical to a "spiritual" ground that underlies a truly mutual relationship.

The power of such spiritual love (with erotic dimensions) is described by psychiatrist Viktor Frankl, survivor of Auschwitz. What gave inmates minute-by-minute courage to go on (to say yes to life despite all) was physical love transformed into spiritual love—the spiritual presence of loved ones who were physically absent (possibly dead). Day after day, almost frozen, exhausted by starvation and backbreaking labor, Frankl carried on a spiritual dialogue with his wife, a dialogue made possible by the physical love they had experienced.

Human eros finds its origin in divine eros, the desire for God who is the ultimate ground of our whole existence.

20

JUDGMENT
Why Believe in Hell?

I N 1995, I SPENT TIME IN A SMALL SEASIDE VILLAGE ON the island of Korcula in Croatia. The terms "judgment" and "hell" were the last words that come to mind in that undisturbed hamlet on the Adriatic coast. There everybody knew everybody, the locals were friendly to strangers even if we couldn't communicate very well, the wine was cheap, and olives, oranges, lemons and figs were homegrown. The terraced hillside gardens above the brilliant blue-green sea presented an idyllic scene. "Heaven" seemed a more appropriate metaphor.

And yet, a dark shadow hung over this place. People were depressed and suffering economically from four years of war with Serbia, ever since Croatia seceded from the Yugoslav federation in 1991. Incredible atrocities had been committed on both sides. The cycle of violence in the Balkans had gone on for centuries, making it difficult to know what justice means. Some fair-minded intellectuals, whom I had known since 1977 through my involvement with a course on the "Future of religion" in Dubrovnik, had become embittered and filled with hatred against the "enemy." Some had succumbed to alcohol and despair.

Others—I think especially of two wonderful elderly women, one of whom lost all her possessions (except for the house itself) to pillage by soldiers and neighbors—had remained sane, philosophical, and remarkably fair in their analysis of the situation, blaming both sides and calling for forgiveness.

It is in such situations of evil and violence that the theological notions of judgment and hell take on meaning. Liberals are embarrassed with the doctrines of the end times, either because these doctrines don't seem to make sense, or because they don't believe that human beings are really that bad. Fundamentalists tend to reduce the notion of hell to a literalistic concept of a place in time and space that burns forever and ever. Neither liberals nor fundamentalists do justice to these important doctrines.

For one thing, people really are that bad. There is no limit to the depths of depravity and barbarism that human beings can sink to in a time of crisis. We are all capable of unimaginable evil. The reason we need to talk about God's wrath is because sin and evil must be taken seriously, while leaving punishment and vengeance in God's hands (Romans 12:19).

For another thing, to relegate hell to a particular place in the universe is too easy. And to ask, as moderns are prone to do, "Is there really a place called 'Hell?'" is to miss the whole point of this indispensable teaching. The final vindication of innocent victims, and the settling of accounts do not rest with the arbitrary will of human beings. God is the ultimate judge.

It is interesting that the Gospel of Matthew, known for the Sermon on the Mount, the basis of the Mennonite doctrine of love and nonresistance, is also full of references to hell and eternal punishment (5:22, 5:29, 10:28, 18:9, 25:30, 25:41). Frequently the call to human love is juxtaposed with references to divine judgment. The same verse that calls for reconciliation between people threatens hell for calling someone a fool (Matthew 5:22). In a passage about the value of all life, even that of a single sparrow, and about God numbering the hairs of our head, we are called to fear him who can kill both soul and body in hell (Matthew 10:28, Luke 12:4).

What can one make of such paradoxes? To begin with, this language about the future, heaven, judgment, and hell is figurative language, the language of parable. "Jesus told the crowds all these things in parables; without a parable he told them nothing" (Matthew 13:34). The biblical image of the "lake of fire" with its "weeping and gnashing of teeth" is meant to convey figuratively the seriousness of sin, and the conviction that evil cannot be committed with impunity. Nor is it up to human beings to pass final judgment.

But this figurative language points to a reality that we cannot yet comprehend. At one point Jesus says to his disciples, "I have said these things to you in figures of speech. The hour is coming when I will no longer speak to you in figures [the German says *Bilder*—pictures] but tell you plainly of the Father" (John 16:25).

Sometimes figures (pictures) can illumine deeper realities for us. At other times they can distance us from real life, as television does—we see life pass before us via floating images. We are called beyond figurative speech to engagement with life and concrete existence. To leave final arbitration to God does not absolve us of responsibility for human action.

In his *Letters and Papers from Prison,* German theologian Dietrich Bonhoeffer wrote about human beings "come of age." No longer ought we to rely on God to do everything; we must become "worldly," and live as though God were not to exist. We should take responsibility for the struggle against evil, he said. How far he was willing to go testifies to his courage and "martyrdom."

On April 6, 1995, I visited Flossenburg, the concentration camp where, in the early hours of April 9, 1945, Bonhoeffer was hanged with other conspirators for their involvement in the unsuccessful attempt on Hitler's life in 1944. Bonhoeffer sacrificed his pacifist convictions and his life in the struggle for human dignity and justice. And yet, admirable and understandable as it was, Bonhoeffer's decision is difficult to reconcile with our understanding of Christ's call to love of enemy and nonviolent action. Did Bonhoeffer usurp the role of God? Even that judgment must be left to God.

21

LIFE EVERLASTING
Gazing into Heaven

R APTURE! FOR MOST PEOPLE THIS TERM CONJURES UP images of extreme pleasure—sexual ecstasy or an intense aesthetic experience. For some, rapture is "that great meeting in the air," the title of a gospel song I used to sing. In this vision, Christ comes down from above and is met halfway by the saints who in their white robes float heavenward (based on Luke 17 and 21, Mark 13, and Matthew 24). Left behind in a state of utter chaos are all those not washed in the blood of the Lamb.

I still remember the dread that overcame me whenever I saw the picture of the rapture in my grandmother's kitchen. Would I be left behind?

Bizarre images connected with the end times—antichrist, tribulation, apocalypse, and the thousand years—have piqued our imaginations and sometimes skewed the church's understanding of the end of history.

Early Anabaptists were preoccupied with apocalyptic and prophetic literature (e.g. Daniel and Revelation) and the end of the world: Thomas Müntzer's preaching, Melchoir Hoffman's predictions about the coming of the kingdom in Strasbourg, the Münster Anabaptists' uprising in an attempt to usher in the New Jerusalem. One thinks also of Claas Epp and his followers who trekked to central Asia in the nineteenth century to meet the returning Christ.

The doctrine of the end times was at the heart of the Anabaptist movement. This theme manifested itself in different ways—sometimes escapist (giving up responsibility for the world), sometimes transformist (inspiring greater involvement in the world).

The Bible speaks about the end times—hell, heaven, judgment, resurrection, eternal life, kingdom of God—in a variety of spatial and temporal images. These biblical images are frequently inconsistent, if taken literally. For this reason, Jesus speaks in parables when describing the kingdom of God.

It is impossible to get any spatially coherent picture of biblical eschatology. "Eternal life" usually refers to inner space, a new way of being, rather than a place where we live forever and ever (Matthew 19-18, 1 John 5:13, 20). "Heaven," on the other hand, connotes that which is beyond us or "above" us (Psalm 139:8, Mark 10:19). Jesus "ascends" to heaven and "the rapture," from the Latin word *rapere,* means "being carried away in body or spirit."

On occasion, heaven is seen not as an alternative to earthly existence, but as a futuristic concept in which a new heaven and a new earth replace the old (2 Peter 3:13, Matthew 5:18, 13:31, Luke 21:33). The best-known biblical passage in this regard is Revelation 21, which imagines the New Jerusalem as a holy city coming down from above. The saints are not whisked away from the earth, but God comes down to dwell with all of creation.

This New Jerusalem is pictured as an ancient walled city with twelve gates named after the twelve tribes of Israel, and twelve foundations named after the twelve apostles. The Jewish vision of the messianic age and New Testament eschatology are brought together in the final chapters of the Bible. God (Yahweh) and the Lamb (Christ) are the Alpha and Omega, the beginning and end of this new heaven and earth.

How is one to sort out all these allegorical representations of the end times and the diversity of spatial images: inward, upward, downward, forward, backward? Sequential time and bounded space seem to have been suspended. Maybe biblical language about the end time is not so far from the popular imagination of our time. We, too, are fascinated with imagining other worlds, with treks among the stars, with fantasies where time and space are transformed into dimensions beyond our experience. Why do we have so much difficulty with biblical language? Biblical beliefs about the end times, like all imaginative thought, emerge from human experience, often in the face of persecution, suffering, or death.

The doctrine of the resurrection evolved over a period of almost 2,000 years, from the earliest Old Testament belief in a shadowy underworld (Hades or Sheol) where everyone went (1 Samuel 28:8–9, Job 7:9, Psalm 6:4–5), to immortality through one's children (2 Samuel 18:18), to the physical resurrection of the Jewish people (Ezekiel 37:1–4, Daniel 12:1–4), to the resurrection of the body of Christ (1 Corinthians 15:12–19), to the general resurrection.

To say that beliefs develop over a long period of time does not relativize their truth—it means that they have connections with real life. Because our religious beliefs are so profoundly entwined with our existence, and because human existence never remains static, the doctrinal metaphors and symbols we use to express divine truth also change.

Behind all the biblical images connected with the end time is the impulse toward transformation, conversion, and liberation of present existence. To speculate about when, where, and how this or that will happen is to miss this point.

The first Christians believed that they were already experiencing the resurrection (rapture) of the spirit and the body of which Christ's resurrection was the "first fruit" (1 Corinthians 15:20). All of creation would someday experience this same restoration and reunion. It's in this spirit that the two men in white robes say to those staring upward after the ascending Christ: "People of Galilee, why do you stand looking into heaven?" (Acts 1:11). Get on with life!

At the heart of all parables about the end time and the kingdom of God is a call to human responsibility in this life. The bodily departure of Christ makes possible his return in a new form—as a transforming power (the Spirit) within us and within the world.

THE FAITHFUL CHURCH
Tolerance, Exclusion,
or Forbearance?

W E TEND TO THINK THAT THE STREAM IS PUREST AT ITS source, when it first bubbles out of the earth. As it begins to flow, it gathers runoff and merges with other streams, becoming muddier and more polluted.

As Mennonites, we also tend to think that the earliest church must have been the purest. As the church spread and gained more members, especially from the powerful classes, it lost its early clarity and commitment. If we could only rediscover Jesus as he really was. If we could only recapture the enthusiasm of Pentecost and the unwavering faith of the martyrs.

But think of the stream again. As it flows on, tumbling over rapids and waterfalls, the water may actually become purified in its interaction with rocks and air. The church is the ongoing presence of Christ in the world, moving through history. The church is not most faithful at its start but becomes faithful as it carries out the mission that Jesus gave it: "Go out and make disciples of all nations." In fact,

Jesus encouraged his followers not to be fixated on him: "It is to your advantage that I go away. . . . I still have many things to say to you, but you cannot bear them now. When the Spirit of truth comes, he will guide you into all the truth" (John 16:7, 12–13). On this basis, beliefs themselves can be said to develop over time.

To be faithful does not mean that the church seeks first and foremost to be perfect. It is to follow in Jesus' ministry of healing, salvation, and reconciliation—both in its own ranks and in the broken world in which it exists. In some ways, the church becomes more and more faithful as it becomes deeper and muddier, as it interacts with the rocks and the rapids of life. It is this idea that first is not necessarily better that attracts me to the later writings in the New Testament—the epistles of Timothy, Titus, James, Peter, John, and Jude. Here one gets a sense of the challenges the church faces after Jesus and the apostles are gone.

Today, Mennonite churches are involved in an intense debate about who's in and who's out. What is the basis for membership? Should individuals or congregations be excluded for disagreement over issues such as homosexuality? In an earlier period the issues were joining the military, divorce and remarriage, and ordination of women. The high price Mennonites have placed on discipleship, on living a morally upright life in accordance with Jesus' life and teachings, has been a preoccupation with church purity.

We know there have never been perfect Christians. The earliest followers of Jesus were ordinary human beings seeking salvation. There was infighting and jealousy. Thomas had severe doubts. Judas betrayed Jesus. All of them forsook

Jesus in the face of danger. Later, Paul got into fights with fellow workers and church leaders. Early churches of Gentile converts, especially the Corinthians, were torn apart by immorality and factionalism.

This is not the picture of holiness and purity. Paul's many pronouncements against living according to the "flesh" and his repeated call for unity would suggest that carnal living and disunity were precisely the problems plaguing the early church. And yet, something powerful was going on—there was a conviction that God had been revealed in Jesus. Miraculous healings were taking place, forgiveness and salvation were available, and the Spirit of truth and love was at work in their midst.

In 1 Timothy 1:3–17, the primary concern is sound doctrine or teaching. There were a lot of frauds around who were occupied with "endless genealogies," "speculations" and "meaningless talk." They were teaching the law without knowing the true nature of the law. The early church was being bombarded with philosophies and moral restrictions not consistent with the teachings of Christ, not in accord with "love that comes from a pure heart, a good conscience, and sincere faith."

One of the reasons the early church developed its leadership offices and its confessions was to preserve the core message of Jesus and the apostles. The church is always tempted to get lost in vain discussion, endless genealogies, speculations, attempting to teach the divine law without knowing the true nature of the law.

What is the true nature of this law? Look at 1 John 4:1–12. The problem here is the diverse spirits and "false prophets" that are getting a foothold in the community of believers. Christians are told to test these spirits by a single criterion: whether they confess "that Jesus Christ has come in the flesh." Any other spirit is wrong and of the anti-Christ. This sounds like a harsh and intolerant standard, especially in our age, which emphasizes openness to other faiths and points of view. In fact, this confession is a liberating one. It is not some abstract formula, such as "I believe in Jesus Christ," or "You can't get to heaven if you don't follow these rules." No, the content of this confession is that love has come in the flesh, in human form.

First John 4:7–9 says it this way: "Beloved, let us love one another, because love is from God; everyone who loves is born of God and knows God. Whoever does not love does not know God, for God is love. God's love was revealed among us in this way: God sent his only Son into the world so that we might live through him."

The core confession of the early church is the following:

1. God is love and this is the most profound thing one can say of God.

2. God loves the world.

3. Jesus Christ is the manifestation of God's love.

4. God forgives our sins, and therefore . . .

5. We ought to love one another.

This is the gospel, the right spirit, the true doctrine, the foundation of the church. This is "the way, the truth and the life." This confession is the basis for church membership, practice, and discipline.

Tolerance. One might draw the conclusion from this confession that we ought to promote unlimited tolerance in society and in the church. Wrong. Tolerance is an unbiblical and un-Christian concept. It applies in a polytheistic society where all religions leave each other alone and do not try to win converts.

In the third century, Roman emperor Diocletian persecuted Christians for not being tolerant. He wanted a state with religious freedom and saw Christians as a threat to this vision because, unlike the Jews, they were trying to convert others to their faith. Today we live in a similar polytheistic situation in which we are expected to tolerate almost any lifestyle, viewpoint, or religious spirit, even within the church. This kind of "tolerance" is inconsistent with the Christian gospel.

It has often been pointed out that the early Anabaptists were among the first to promote religious toleration. Menno Simons, for example, appealed to the magistrates for tolerance. But the Anabaptists were not the first to do this—the pagan emperor Diocletian already called for religious toleration in the third century. Furthermore, the Anabaptists did not mean by toleration what Diocletian meant or what is meant today—let people believe what they want and leave them alone. What they meant was much closer to what I call "forbearance."

Exclusion. As soon as we examine more closely the command to love, we realize it is not as simple as we might think. The essence of the Jewish law is the Shema: "You shall love the Lord your God with all your heart, and with all your soul, and with all your might" and "You shall love your neighbor as yourself" (Deuteronomy 6:5, Leviticus 19:18, Matthew 22:37-39). Law is the structure of love, giving love its content.

When Jesus speaks of loving God and neighbor, he is not negating all the Jewish laws, but is giving us the deepest reason for them. When Jesus says he came not to abolish the law but to fulfill it (Matthew 5:17-20), he is in effect saying that love is not an alternative to law but the reason for good law.

In the church's struggle to remain faithful to the law it has often forgotten that "law is based on love" not "love on the law." In the church we ought not to love someone because she keeps the law, but because the law is love. When we get lost in endless disputes about right behavior and purity of obedience to certain rules as the basis for church membership we betray the very basis of those laws: love of God and the other.

But there is a place for church discipline, for exclusion from the community of faith. Jesus' injunction to Peter and the disciples (Matthew 16 and 18) gives the keys (the right to bind and loose) to the church. What is the legitimate basis for exclusion? I would propose that just cause for exclusion from church membership is not breaking a law as such—it is breaking the command to love God and neighbor that is the basis of law. To put it bluntly—it is for "hatred" of God and the other that one is to be excluded (or, more accurately, that one excludes oneself) from the community of love.

Forbearance. Exclusion has been far too frequently practiced by the church, especially by the Mennonite community. My own grandfather, a faithful minister for many years, was unjustly banned by the church he had served. Church discipline (especially exclusion) is justified only in the rarest of cases, when the very core of the church's confession is at stake.

Should those who live a "sinful" life be excluded? It would appear from Matthew 18:15ff. that intentional sinful behavior is just cause for "redemptive" exclusion. What is noteworthy, however, is that this text does not spell out what constitutes "sin," stating only "if another member of the church sins against you." In short, in this case the problem has to do with relationships between members, and only after repeated attempts at reconciliation have failed is exclusion to be exercised.

In the case of homosexuality, the church's acceptance or even blessing of homosexual unions (made with the same promise of fidelity as heterosexual unions) becomes extremely complex. The complexity rests in the fact that church members are divided on whether "sin" applies here. In this case, it seems to me that the primary issue for membership is not what type of sexual union is practiced, although that is an important theological issue, but whether either party in the debate is endangering the very foundation of church membership—confession that in Jesus Christ, God's love is manifest.

When both sides with integrity confess this Jesus, exclusion is unjustified. It then becomes a church polity issue—finding a way to reconcile differences provisionally while continuing to seek theological consensus. Given the church's current understanding, this would mean: not "blessing" same-sex unions but in certain circumstances "forbearing" them. And it would also mean forbearance from homosexual Christians of the church's struggle to understand homosexuality in the light of biblical teaching.

A challenge to the confession existed in the German church during the Hitler period. In May 1934, the "Confessing Church" excluded the pro-Hitler members, known as the German Christians, from the true church, calling them heretics. This drastic decision was made because the German Christians wanted to ban Jews who had converted to Christianity from being ministers in the church.

When the church exercises such extreme discipline it does so at great peril for it knows it is fallible and could be wrong. It knows that it will be judged by the same standard it applies to others. Forbearance is not tolerance of whatever people believe or do. Forbearance is the biblical notion that as we judge others, so we will be judged, that we should first remove the beam in our own eye before trying to remove the splinter in our neighbor's eye.

Forbearance is the Christian belief that we ought to bear each other's burdens, weaknesses, shortcomings, handicaps, and sins. It is based on the biblical understanding of God— a God whose love, mercy, and compassion far outweigh the word of judgment, a God who loves the world and bears its shortcomings, whose goal is to reconcile all things.

There is a fundamental difference between the Christian notion of forbearance and the pagan notion of tolerance. With forbearance, one holds strong commitments and tries to convince others to share them, while learning to live with those who differ from us. Within the Judeo-Christian tradition this translates into loving God with all our heart, mind and soul, and the other as oneself. Within the Christian church, this translates into the confession that in Jesus the Christ this love of God and the other has come in the flesh and continues in the life of the church.

23

THE CORPORATE CHURCH
A Ship of Fools

I N 1946, AMERICAN AUTHOR KATHERINE ANNE Porter published her classic novel, *Ship of Fools*. It is the story of a shipload of passengers on a 1931 voyage from Mexico to the doomed Germany. On board are a motley group of some 1,000 people from all walks of life: lovers, widows, families, Germans returning home, Swiss, Spaniards, Swedes, Cubans, Mexicans, and Americans. Their sordid relationships on board are described in great detail. They are all "fools," unaware of the catastrophe awaiting them in Europe. Porter was inspired by the sixteenth-century moral allegory by Sabastian Brant, *Das Narrenschiff,* which sees the ship of this world on a journey to eternity. We are all passengers on that ship.

The voyage to eternity is a very old archetype for the transitory nature of life. It is also part of the biblical story. However, in the biblical narrative, the voyage is not a meaningless journey into the abyss. Rather, it takes place in the context of a grand vision: the creation of a perfect world, its fall into death and darkness, and its final redemption and resurrection. The passengers on the biblical voyage also appear by all human standards to be fools. But, in fact, they possess the divine revelation of the true nature of the universe and cosmic history.

In the Old Testament, the ship allegory comes in the form of Noah's ark and the great flood (Genesis 6–8). It is an ancient saga, probably edited into an account of human origins by Jewish authors sometime around the fifth century B.C.E. It was their allegorical way of accounting for their view of the world: divine origins, creation, the origin of evil and human sin, survival of the human race, and the birth and destiny of the Jewish people in the midst of all other peoples. Using highly personified language for God, the authors describe the flood in terms of divine punishment and Noah's ark as a divine rescue operation. Only a small remnant of people and animals survive. Noah's building of the ark on dry land is foolish by pagan standards—he and his family are the laughingstock of the doomed world around them, as the Jews themselves must have appeared foolish to surrounding cultures. (Sometimes it's difficult, of course, to distinguish between "fools" and "madmen." In *Dust Ship Glory,* Mennonite novelist Andreas Schroeder narrates the true story of such a mad [or maybe not-so-mad] man who builds a huge ship on the parched Saskatchewan prairies in the 1930s.)

The Jewish ark allegory, however, only makes sense in the context of a larger vision, one driven by an unshakable conviction that there is something objective going on in the universe. Although the saga of Genesis 1–11 is compiled by Jewish authors, it is a universal story of fall from perfection and rescue of a few not-so-righteous individuals who begin the slide into wickedness and violence all over again. The specifically Jewish story begins only in Genesis 12, as part of that universal narrative. I don't need to recount the subsequent dramatic rescue of the Hebrew people from Egypt, the giving of the Torah, the coming of the judges, kings, prophets, and the Jewish hope for the final rescue by a Messiah. The Messianic Age would restore all things to their original glory—lambs and lions would lie together, peace and justice would reign, and the whole cosmos would be redeemed.

This grand narrative is presupposed by the early Christians who claim that in Jesus of Nazareth, God has inaugurated this Messianic rescue operation.

The New Testament ship allegory is Paul's voyage to Rome, told in the last two chapters of Acts. It has been suggested by Robert C. Tannehill in his book, *The Narrative Unity of Luke–Acts: A Literary Interpretation,* that the ship and its voyage is an allegory for the early church within the Roman Empire. It is a remarkable story.

A common theme of Luke and Acts, generally considered to be written by the same person, is "universal salvation." In Luke 3:5–6 we read: *"Every* valley shall be filled, and *every* mountain and hill shall be made low, and the crooked shall be made straight, and the rough ways made smooth; and *all flesh* shall see the salvation of God" (italics mine). The book of Acts from beginning to end is concerned with universalizing the message of salvation to include both Jews and Gentiles. This is the central purpose of Paul's missionary journeys, his famous defense speeches before Jewish and Roman authorities, and his final journey to Rome.

The most interesting exploration of this theme is Acts 27:1–28:16. The narrator portrays the journey of the ship through the stormy sea as a grand metaphor for the Christian church in relation to the larger world. God, via Paul, promises that the whole mixed company aboard the ship will survive. The chief protagonists of the story are the centurion Julius and his soldiers, the sailors, and, of course, Paul himself. Each of the crew contributes to their final rescue, but especially Paul through his interventions at critical points, with the cooperation of Julius. A friendship develops right from the start between the non-Christian Julius and Paul, a relationship of trust that results in the rescue of all aboard the ship, most of them pagans who worship other gods. There is a deliberate attempt by the author of Acts to portray the pagan Roman world as an instrument of divine providence.

The meal on the ship, in which everyone participates, has eucharistic overtones. Paul says: "Therefore I urge you to take some food, for it will help you survive; for none of you will lose a hair from your heads." And when he had said this, "he took bread; and giving thanks to God in the presence of all, he broke it and began to eat" (Acts 27:34-35). The story ends with the ship being destroyed but all 276 persons, including prisoners, safely escaping to land, which turns out to be the island of Malta.

The most remarkable thing about the story is, first, that the ship itself (as an allegory for the institutional church) does not survive but the people do. Second, Paul makes no reference to faith in Christ as a precondition for rescue (salvation), and third, the pagan centurion and sailors play an indispensable role in the drama of God's saving design for the passengers, symbolizing all of humanity. There is no indication that Paul preached Christ to the passengers or the peoples of Malta—God's saving work in this case does not seem to depend on the rejection or acceptance of the message. While the case for "universal salvation" (every single person will be saved whether they believe or not) cannot be inferred from this story, some kind of universality is implied. True, human agency is critical in reaching the goal, but it is an agency that is not autonomous but derivative of divine agency.

Even the "barbarian" islanders of Malta with their religious superstition (they think of Paul as a god when he is not harmed by the viper) show warm hospitality to the entourage. Robert Tannehill writes, "The narrative undermines any tendency for Christians to regard the world in general as hostile and evil."

Paul stays on the island for three months and, like Jesus, performs many miracles of healing, but we are not told that he preaches to the Maltans. They are allowed to remain pagan, demonstrating once again the cooperation between pagan society and Christians in contributing to the divine purpose.

Despite this positive portrayal of pagans and Gentiles, Paul remains a prisoner, and his unsuccessful mission to the Jewish community in Rome ends the narrative of Luke-Acts with an unresolved tension. There is no evidence that the promise that "all flesh shall see the salvation of God," promised in Luke 3:6, is anywhere near to being fulfilled. Like Jesus, Paul's mission ends in rejection by his people and in suffering. There is a tragic and ironic tone to the end of

Acts: the Gentiles are ready to hear but the Jews are deaf. We are not told whether Paul finally did appear before the Emperor; we are not told about his martyrdom. The question of the acceptance or rejection of the Messianic hope by the Jewish people remains unresolved.

Other biblical texts emphasize personal responsibility in salvation, but here in Acts the role of the individual is secondary. There is something much larger going on and individuals, even Paul and the captain, are but instruments in a divine plan. As Mennonites, we have emphasized the critical importance of individual decision and responsibility. The church, we believe, is made up of those who voluntarily commit themselves to a community of gathered believers, and receive baptism upon personal confession of faith as a sign of this decision. But let's remember that the church is not simply a sum of its parts. The church is something much larger: it is a transitory witness to what God has already done and is already doing in the world—redeeming it. Each congregation is but one little, imperfect expression of this witness.

Alistair MacLeod's wonderful novel, *No Great Mischief* (2001), and tells the story of the MacDonald family who in the eighteenth century emigrate from Scotland to Cape Breton, Nova Scotia. It's an incredibly close family in some respects, but emotionally and physically torn apart in others. What holds them together is not personal choice but their common origin and fate. In one passage, the men go into the forest to cut timber for the skidway for their boat. In the middle of a spruce grove, they find a perfect tree, tall and straight. They notch it and saw it with their bucksaw.

When they're finished, nothing happens. The top branches of the tree are so intertwined with others that it just remains standing. There is no way it could fall or be removed without cutting down the whole forest. So that's where it remains to this day. No one would know by looking at the grove that there is a lone tree standing in the middle, cut off from its roots.

MacLeod also tells of family members taking out a photo album to look at pictures of their deceased parents. They find no pictures of their parents alone, only as part of the extended clan. So they decide to ask a photo studio to isolate the parents from the rest and enlarge their faces for a separate photograph. But as the photograph became larger the faces became more blurred and indistinct. To isolate them and to bring them closer is to lose them. In the end, they just leave the parents as part of the whole family.

To me, these two stories illustrate profoundly the nature of the church. It's really a reversal of what Mennonites often think the church to be. We say, "If only we would have individuals more committed to the church, we would have a vibrant community; a dissenting, wayward or unbelieving brother or sister should shape up or leave." But isn't it the other way around? The church is the corporate body of Christ, the corporate witness to what God is doing universally. It holds within its ranks pastors and skeptics, prophets and doubters, prisoners and soldiers, eccentrics and fools.

Our term "community" does not do justice to this objective, universal reality of divine providence and agency. To emphasize this objective character of the church, one might even say that the church believes corporately on behalf of those who have difficulty believing and living right, on behalf of all of us imperfect, individual members. The church exists vicariously for the sake of the world. I'm tempted to say it is almost irrelevant what you or I believe as individuals. This is not to minimize the truth that each individual has personal responsibility and intrinsic value before God. It is to emphasize the corporate nature of the body of Christ. Ultimately what matters is not individual belief, but our corporate witness to what God is doing in the world.

24

SOLDIERS OR MARTYRS?
Laying Down One's Life for Another

I N THE 1998 MOVIE, *SAVING PRIVATE RYAN,* THE HIGH command decides to risk the lives of eight men in order to find one soldier. It's the dramatic story of a dangerous mission in France during World War II to rescue the only remaining son of four brothers gone off to war. The goal is to return this son safely to his mother so she will at least have one left. In the end, most of the men sent on the mission are killed, including the commander, but Ryan is saved.

In the meantime, we are forced to view the carnage of war. What keeps the commander going is the conviction that for every soldier that dies under his command, at least ten people will somewhere be saved, the belief that his soldiers are laying down their lives for others in a worthy cause. War is perhaps the clearest example of how individuals, even in our decadent, narcissistic western world, can still transcend their self-interest and fight for a common good, a higher cause. But is it really the common good? Is the higher cause a worthy one?

Mennonites have always been confused about Remembrance Day. Should we participate? Should we wear a poppy in remembrance of all those brave soldiers—many of them young people in their late teens and early twenties—who died for us? Even if we reject all war as a means of achieving a higher good? On Remembrance Day I wear both a poppy and a Mennonite Central Committee peace pin as a way of saying, "Yes." This day is a time when we can remember all suffering of the past, by combatants and non-combatants who served for what they believed to be true. Suffering is suffering, no matter where or how it occurs, and God is in the midst of suffering. The poppy represents for me this "weeping for those who weep" for lost loved ones, and the peace symbol represents the refusal to participate in the killing machine that causes such suffering. It is my way of saying "No," I will not compromise, I refuse to participate in the cycle of violence, no matter how worthy the cause appears. I do this because I am a follower of Jesus, and Jesus taught us to turn the other cheek, to walk the second mile, to love the enemy, not to shed blood.

The church has a very dark record in this regard. From early on, Christians have disagreed on how to read the Scriptures on the use of coercion, violence, and war as a means of achieving justice. It is a complex issue with no easy answer.

1. Many texts in the Old Testament, and some in the New, suggest that God is a kind of Holy Warrior who in some cases uses war, and even commands war, in a holy cause. The story of the exodus from Egypt and conquering the land of Canaan in the Old Testament, and sections of

Revelation in the New Testament, are examples of this view of God. There are those in the history of the Christian church who, on the basis of texts like these, have defended holy wars and crusades against infidels. Examples are the Crusades of Christians against Muslims in the Middle Ages, revolutionary wars in the Reformation (even by some Anabaptists), and "liberation wars" in this century.

2. Other biblical texts would appear to suggest how war can be fought under certain conditions and according to certain rules. In Deuteronomy 20, the Israelites are given rules for when they can fight and what they may and may not do in war. Romans 13:1-7 tells us that rulers are ordained by God to bear the sword to punish/restrain evil and reward/protect the good. Christians are to be obedient to them.

In the fourth century, after the Roman Empire had become Christian, the theologian St. Augustine developed what has come to be called the Just War theory. Ever since, the dominant attitude of the Christian church has been that under certain conditions war can be justified as a necessary evil. Augustine was fully convinced that all killing is wrong, a sin against the teachings of Jesus, but his reasoning went like this: We live in a fallen, imperfect, and sinful world where coercion and even violence are required to maintain law and order, to keep the world from becoming even worse. Only in the eternal kingdom of God will there be perfect peace. In the meantime, we ought never to participate in any violence individually, but only when a legitimate authority (as in Romans 13) declares it necessary. When we do fight we ought never to kill another out of vengeance but always in an attitude of love (as taught in the

Sermon on the Mount), asking for forgiveness, and always only as a last resort for the sake of restoring justice. Innocent people (noncombatants) should never be killed.

The problem with this kind of reasoning is that it has been used to defend virtually every war in the West since then, including those in the twentieth century: World War I, World War II, the Korean War, the Vietnam War, the Gulf War, the war against Afghanistan, and now Iraq.

For this reason there have been Christians throughout the ages who have said no to Just War. There is no war that is really just. There is no killing, whether by individuals or by soldiers in a state-declared war, that can be justified on the basis of Jesus' teaching. Already in the Old Testament, the Messiah is understood as someone who does not fight, but as a suffering servant who dies on behalf of others. Christians who protest war are often wrongly called "pacifists." They are not pacifists in any "passivist" sense, but believe that the overriding message of the Bible, including the life, work, and teachings of Jesus Christ, is the gospel of peace and reconciliation through self-giving, suffering love for and on behalf of others. There is a general scholarly belief (although not consensus) that Christians up to the end of the second century were for the most part against all shedding of blood. With the conversion of Constantine, when Christians became rulers and took on responsibility for running the world, this changed. But there has been throughout history a small minority of Christians who have kept alive this earliest form of radical Christian nonviolence: some of the monastic orders in the Middle Ages, the Waldensians from the thirteenth century on, some Anabaptists and Mennonites from the time of the Reformation,

Quakers from the seventeenth century on, and a growing number of Catholics and Protestants in the twentieth century. These Christians do not claim that they are the only Christians, but that it is their calling to "not go along with," to, as Bonhoeffer put it, "put a spoke in the wheel of the cycle of violence," no matter how worthy the cause may appear. In a sense, they are pacifists on behalf of others.

As followers of Jesus, we too are called "to lay our lives down for others" the way he did. In October 2002, I helped to host a group of Muslim clergy and academics from Iran. They were here in Toronto for a dialogue between Shi'ite Muslims and Mennonite Christians on the challenges of the modern world for our religious communities. On Saturday night we visited a mosque in Toronto and on Sunday morning we attended a worship service at the Tavistock Mennonite Church. In the afternoon we went to an Old Order Mennonite farm and schoolhouse. One of the Muslims was so impressed with the simple lifestyle of these Old Order Mennonites that he exclaimed: "These people when they die will go straight on an express to paradise."

During the visit to the mosque, I was asked to say a few words about what Christians believe about Jesus. Muslims believe that their twelfth Imam (leader) did not die but was transformed and will return with Jesus to set up a perfect kingdom of peace and justice. They believe Jesus was a great prophet, but they don't believe that he was God, nor that he was crucified. In fact, I have been told that Muslims have no doctrine of "substitutionary atonement"—that is, that someone like Jesus had to be sacrificed for the sins of the people. Muslims have a strong sense of their own sin, but they believe that God the all-merciful and all-compassionate One forgives them directly. His love and grace is not mediated through anyone. This is a fundamental difference between Islam and Christianity. Central to Christian faith is the atonement, the belief that God reconciles the world through Christ's suffering on the cross, and that we as Christians continue this reconciliation through self-sacrificial love. We tend to forget this central aspect of the gospel in our afflu-ent lives. It is during times of war that we are forced to remember this teaching, to make a decision whether to lay down our lives by fighting as soldiers or in some other way. If this "some other way" is easier than what soldiers do, then it is not the way of Jesus.

The Muslim terrorists who bombed the World Trade Center believed they were martyrs for their faith. Mohammed Atta, believed to be the mastermind, probably wrote the letter that spells out the motivations behind their actions. For them, this terrorist act was martyrdom for a higher cause, a form of obedience to Allah: "There is no god but God, and Muhammad is the messenger of God." This act would guarantee their life in paradise. Many Muslims condemn this act as going against the true teaching of the Qur'an, reminding us that the Qu'ran also says: "If you save one life you save the whole world, if you take one life you take the life of all." This comes close to the Christian notion of substitution. Although my Muslim friends tell me there is no equivalent within Islam to what we call pacifism, there is a strong emphasis on peace and justice in the Qu'ran. And we have to remember constantly that Christianity too has committed its share of terrorism and violence in the name of God, probably more so than Islam. In both terrorist mar-tyrdom and nonviolent martyrdom one lays down one's life for another. But in one case one does so by taking the life of another and in the other by refusing to do so.

I end with a text from the *War Requiem* by Benjamin Britten. Britten, a twentieth-century composer who was also a pacifist, wrote the *War Requiem* not only as a tribute to all those who died in World War II, but as a protest against all war. He juxtaposed parts of the Roman Catholic Mass for the Dead with words of the young English poet, Wilfred Owen, who died in the trenches just before the end of World War I. In one of the most dramatic moments of the Requiem, Owen retells the story of Abram's sacrifice of Isaac:

> So Abram rose, and clave the wood, and went,
> And took the fire with him, and a knife.
> And as they sojourned both of them together,
> Isaac the first-born spake and said, My Father,
> Behold the preparations, fire and iron,
> But where the lamb for this burnt-offering?
> Then Abram bound the youth with belts and straps,
> And builded parapets and trenched there,
> And stretched forth the knife to slay his son.
> When lo! An angel called him out of heaven,
> Saying, Lay not thy hand upon the lad,
> Neither do anything to him. Behold,
> A ram, caught in a thicket by its horns;
> Offer the Ram of Pride instead of him.
> But the old man would not so,
> but slew his son, —
> And half the seed of Europe, one by one.

In the story of Abram's almost sacrifice of his son Isaac we have the ultimate revelation of divine will. Abram is faced with a choice: to kill or not to kill. He decides not to kill. The ram in the thicket becomes the scapegoat for the sins and violence of the people. The ram lays down its life for Abram's seed. The scapegoat becomes an important symbol of substitution for the Jews, and Christ becomes the scapegoat symbol for Christians. Unfortunately, human beings, including Christians, have not heeded God's command to Abram not to slay one another.

On Remembrance Day, we as Mennonite pacifists are called to weep with those who weep, and remember with those who remember the ones who suffered and died, even for causes we don't agree with. We do this not self-righteously but in great sorrow, taking upon ourselves, as the body of Christ, the sin and guilt of the world. In this way, we participate in the divine process of redemption for a suffering world.

THE AUTHOR

THOMAS SIEBERT

A. JAMES REIMER TEACHES RELIGION AND THEOLOGY AT Conrad Grebel University College, University of Waterloo, in Ontario. He is also on the faculty of the Toronto School of Theology and is Director of the Toronto Mennonite Theological Centre. Reimer has written many articles and numerous books, the most recent being *Mennonites and Classical Theology: Dogmatic Foundations for Christian Ethics.* He has lectured widely both in North America and Europe, including Yugoslavia, on theology in the Nazi period, Mennonite theology, and peace theology. His most recent research is in the area of theology, law, and civil institutions.

Reimer is a member of the Rockway Mennonite Church, Kitchener, Ontario, and is active in teaching and preaching within the Mennonite community. He is married to Margaret Loewen Reimer and they have three children: Christina, Thomas, and Micah.